Operation Exodus

Operation Exodus

Gustav Scheller

with

Jonathan Miles

2011
EDITION

Ebenezer Operation Exodus

Published by:
Ebenezer Emergency Fund International
Ebenezer House
5a Poole Road
Bournemouth, BH5 2QJ
England

ISBN: 978-0-9569448-0-1

Cover pictures: Ebenezer Emergency Fund International
Typeset by CPI Group (UK) Ltd., Croydon, Surrey CR0 4YY
Printed and bound by CPI Group (UK) Ltd, Croydon, CR0 4YY

Contents

The Authors

Gustav Scheller

Gustav Scheller was born in Switzerland in 1929 and was called into the Lord's presence on 18th February 2000. He, with his wife Elsa, came to the UK in 1956 to build up a travel and tour operating company. Gustav also established foreign language schools and at the peak of the company's business had offices in London, Edinburgh, Switzerland and Tokyo. The company received the Queen's Award to Industry for travel and tourism in 1974.

While attending Bible college in the USA in 1982 the Lord revealed to Gustav and Elsa through the prophetic writings that end-time events were inseparably linked with the destiny of the Jewish people, especially His plan and purpose for their return to their ancient homeland. With the challenge of this revelation came the crucial thought that if the Lord could not keep His promises to the Jewish people what was the value of His promises to the Church? He also revealed that the time would come when they would personally be involved with the return of the Jewish people in a practical way. Little did they realize what this would mean! At that time many Jewish people were trapped in the super power known as the USSR. To human thinking it seemed impossible that scriptures promising their return from the 'land of the north' could be fulfilled literally! In 1983 Gustav brought together a group called 'Let My People

Go' (God's command to Pharaoh, through Moses), initially to help organize the meeting with Steve Lightle that is recounted in the book. This ministry sought to bring the plight of the Soviet Jews to the attention of the Church and to teach Christians about the biblical destiny of the Jewish people and God's call to the Gentiles to be involved in their return to their ancient homeland (Isaiah 49:22).

It was during the annual International Prayer Conference in Jerusalem in 1991, when 120 intercessors from many different nations had gathered to intercede for Israel, that the Lord spoke to Gustav and told him that **now** was the time to bring home His people from the disintegrating Soviet Union. It was right in the middle of the first Gulf War and not a time Gustav himself would have chosen! In fact, if ever there was a time that such a word could have been considered inopportune, or even downright foolish, this was it! To the leadership and the intercessors' credit, however, the word was tested in accordance with the Scriptures (1 John 4:1-6) and deemed to be of the Lord. So Operation Exodus was born and Gentile believers worldwide have continued to respond to the challenge to help carry the Jewish people home through prayer and financial support. Many have also served in the former Soviet Union itself. 'Ebenezer' is spoken of in the Book of Samuel and means 'Stone of help' or 'Thus far has the Lord helped us' – and this is the testimony of the Ebenezer Emergency Fund, because without His help we could do nothing.

This new edition of the story of the founding and development of the Ebenezer Emergency Fund includes corrections and an update on the progress of the work. By the dawn of 2007 there should be around 120,000 good reasons to praise the Lord for His faithfulness: the total number of Jewish people Operation Exodus has helped to return to Israel since 1991. At the time of going to press this landmark figure was well in sight.

> *'See, I will beckon to the Gentiles,*
>   *I will lift up My banner to the peoples;*
> *they will bring your sons in their arms*
>   *and carry your daughters on their shoulders.'*
>
> Isaiah 49:22 (NIV)

We know that God has kept every one of His promises to Israel. **He who scattered Israel will gather them and keep them** and bring them back to the Land He has given their forefathers as an everlasting possession.

Jonathan Miles

Jonathan Miles is a journalist who lived in Israel for a number of years and, together with his wife and children, worked with Jewish immigrants and Arab refugees.

Clive Price

Clive Price wrote chapters 9 to 11 for this 20th anniversary edition. Clive serves a number of charities and organisations across Britain and Ireland as a writer, editor and creative consultant.

Dedication

To my precious wife, Elsa, travel companion, prayer partner and wise counsellor. Next to God's grace, you are the best thing that ever happened to me.

To Beverley Hill, trusted and loyal assistant over many years, whose support has been an inspiration to me.

To all the valiant servants of Ebenezer, past and present, who have shown love in action to God's chosen people.

To the many believers who have accompanied us in prayer. Without their faithful intercession Operation Exodus would not have succeeded.

To all those who with their gracious and often sacrificial giving have enabled the Jewish people to return to the Promised Land.

Gustav Scheller
1998

Foreword

To God be the Glory

Sitting in a conference hall in Jerusalem in January 2011 among 200 representatives of Ebenezer Operation Exodus from 30 nations, I was overwhelmed by God's marvellous faithfulness: It was exactly 20 years ago to the day – in January 1991 – when the Lord called Operation Exodus into being. It happened under the most unpleasant circumstances in a bomb shelter but it was God's perfect timing. Out of one man's obedience – Gustav Scheller – He created a worldwide ministry which today has many thousands of faithful and committed brothers and sisters.

As you read through the book, the theme of "impossible" is occurring again and again. Just as in the time of the first Exodus, when Pharaoh didn't want to let the people go, we are experiencing many difficulties in aliyah worldwide today. But just as the king of Egypt finally had to release Israel by God's mighty hand, so too He is working in the same way in these days: Whether His people live in a nation which they have difficulty in leaving, or they live in a country which they do not consider leaving, God is removing obstacles and moving hearts in order to fulfil His amazing promises.

All this is happening to glorify His name but equally so that all the nations will know that He is the Lord. (Ezekiel 36:23-24). The following verses show that when the Jewish people are back in the Promised Land, the God of Israel will restore them completely and spiritually! This will release blessings, never experienced before, to all nations – life from the dead. (Romans 11:15)

This is the fourth edition of the story of Operation Exodus and we witness how God is expanding the ministry and preparing it for the days ahead. In an almost breathtaking manner He has opened doors and provided contacts so that Ebenezer is now working in 46 countries worldwide. Beyond that, international networks have been set up with complementary ministries and with many churches. We sense that now is the time when the body of Christ needs to understand her responsibility to help with God's final restoration of Israel and the Jewish people.

Inviting you to read this unique story, I pray you may recognize that we are currently living in the days of fulfilment of these awe-inspiring prophecies foretold thousands of years ago. The homecoming of the Jews demonstrates God's unchangeable faithfulness to His word. It is part of His ultimate goal to establish His eternal kingdom by His beloved Son, our Lord Jesus and Messiah of Israel. That's the truly exciting blessing to come.

Markus J. Ernst
Chairman
Ebenezer Emergency Fund International

Introduction

To understand this book it is first of all essential to understand God, His nature and character, and His eternal purposes for Israel.

Out of love He **chose** Abraham, Isaac and Jacob, whose name was changed to Israel, and promised them a land of their own (Genesis 12:1; 15:7). It is clearly defined as being *'from the river of Egypt to the great river, the river Euphrates'* (Genesis 15:18). That promise has yet to be fulfilled in its completeness, but one day God will ensure that His covenant is kept in full.

We live in an age of 'equality'. Some people even consider it unfair that God should choose the Jewish people as His special people, or indeed promise them their land for ever. Such a promise was made to no other nation. God also foreknew that they would be in Egypt 400 years and told Abraham so:

> *'Know certainly that your descendants will be strangers in a land that is not theirs, and will serve them and they will afflict them four hundred years.'*
>
> Genesis 15:13

God promised that afterwards they would come out and enter the Promised Land. This was achieved through Moses and is the first exodus. It is important to understand this as God later refers back to it in describing a second exodus, which clearly confirms there are two, one past, one future, i.e. after the prophecy that postdates the first exodus.

When we trace Jewish history it is important to understand God's covenant with the Jewish people, especially the Deuteronomy 28 covenant. It is in two sections. Verses 1–14 describe the blessings of obedience; however, verses 15–68 describe in great detail the consequences of disobedience. History tells us that tragically they disobeyed God's laws. The Israelites therefore experienced the consequences of that choice. Specifically:

> *'And you shall become an astonishment, a proverb, and a byword among all nations where the LORD will drive you.'*
>
> Deuteronomy 28:37

> *'...you shall be plucked from off the land which you go to possess. Then the LORD will scatter you among all peoples, from one end of the earth to the other...'*
>
> Deuteronomy 28:63–64

God's people disobeyed Him many times and caused God's anger to rise up, yet even when He allowed them to go into captivity for a time under Nebuchadnezzar (6th century BC), that exile was both temporary and limited, i.e. to Babylon only. They came back. The second exodus we shall look at later cannot be the Babylonian exile for two very simple reasons.

Firstly, the Jewish people were not scattered all over the earth. They were taken into exile into Babylon.

Secondly, Babylon is **east** of Israel, and the second exodus is from 'the land of the north', and from 'all the countries to which they were scattered'. Moscow, the capital of the old Soviet Union, and now of Russia, lies due north of Israel.

> *'...they shall come together out of the land of the north to the land that I have given as an inheritance to your fathers.'*
>
> Jeremiah 3:18

In AD 70 the Roman Emperor Titus, in response to the Jewish revolt, sacked Jerusalem, resulting in the scattering of many Jewish people. The Second Revolt some 60 years later led to the scattering of those who remained. Remarkably, they maintained their identity for almost 2,000 years, experiencing all the curses of Deuteronomy 28, until God chose to give them back their homeland in accordance with His promises and bring back His chosen people. The State of Israel was miraculously reborn in 1948. It has survived war after war.

Unfortunately, for many centuries the Church has taught that God has abandoned His people and that the Covenant promises to the nation of Israel have passed to the Church. This 'replacement theology' teaches that God's promises to Israel are void and are now the property of the Church. While it remains true that the Church became partakers of the covenants and God's promises, it is nevertheless equally true that God has not, did not and will not ever abandon Israel as His chosen people, even during times of discipline.

The prophet Jeremiah gives Israel the most wonderful promises from the Lord:

> *'Yes, I have loved you with an everlasting love;*
> *Therefore with lovingkindness I have drawn you.*
> *Again I will build you, and you shall be rebuilt.'*
>
> Jeremiah 31:3–4

> *'Behold I will bring them from the north country,*
> *And gather them from the ends of the earth.'*
>
> Jeremiah 31:8

> *'He who scattered Israel will gather him.'*
>
> Jeremiah 31:10

These prophecies have never been fulfilled in full. In order to make the point unequivocally, God links His faithfulness to the very existence of the earth:

> 'Thus says the LORD,
> Who gives the sun for a light by day,
> And the ordinances of the moon and
>   the stars for a light by night...
> If those ordinances depart
> From before Me, says the LORD,
> Then the seed of Israel shall also cease
> From being a nation before me forever.'
>
> Jeremiah 31:35–36

God then repeats it, to emphasize the certainty:

> 'If heaven above can be measured,
> And the foundations of the earth searched out beneath,
> I will also cast off all the seed of Israel
> For all that they have done, says the LORD.'
>
> Jeremiah 31:37

Clearly the sun and moon have not ceased shining in line with God's declaration that Israel will remain a nation before Him for ever.

Down through the years from AD 70 to 1948 Israel remained a nation in God's eyes. Then something happened. In 1947 the United Nations voted to partition Palestine, thus paving the way for the declaration of the State of Israel in May 1948.

The nation was reborn. The Jewish people **were back** in their land, with their own identity, territory and language. It truly was the hand of God. But history has not ceased, nor has opposition to God's purposes in history.

Despite all attempts to strangle the new nation at birth, Israel prevailed, and has done so, despite on-going attempts to destroy her. But God has not finished with His people. The wonder is that He has plans for Israel and is watching over His chosen people. He will bring them back to their land and fulfil every promise made.

There will be a second exodus, bringing His people back from oppression to their homeland. It will be even more significant than the first exodus from Egypt:

> *'"Therefore behold, the days are coming," says the LORD, "that it shall no more be said, 'The LORD lives who brought up the children of Israel from the land of Egypt,' but, 'The LORD lives who brought up the children of Israel from the land of the north and from all the lands where He had driven them.' For I will bring them back into their land which I gave to their fathers."'*
>
> Jeremiah 16:14–15

Firstly, they will come through 'fishing' and encouragement. Afterwards persecution will drive them home. It is plain for all to see that anti-Semitism is increasing. Right now God is allowing a period of grace, or fishing. Gustav's testimony tells but a part of what God is doing and how He is using Operation Exodus, the operational arm of Ebenezer Emergency Fund, to fulfil His purposes. We are witnessing history being made before our very eyes. It is time for the Church to be challenged into action. It is time to love God's chosen people as the prophetic fulfilment of God's plan for their homecoming takes place.

CHAPTER 1

An Amazing Vision

'I am God, and there is none like Me,
Declaring the end from the beginning,
And from ancient times things that are not yet done.'
Isaiah 46:9–10

My first inkling of these strange events came in the dining room of a hotel in the north of England. It was the hour of the evening meal and I took the only unoccupied place. The gentleman opposite me, I learned as we waited for the food to be served, was a doctor and a believer.

'I've just come from Israel,' he told me. My ears pricked up. In that Spring of 1982 my wife Elsa and I had just finished ten weeks of Bible study at the beautiful Christian Retreat in Bradenton, Florida, and our eyes had been opened to God's promises to the Jewish people. I didn't fully understand why, but I had a sense that Elsa and I should go to Israel. I had come aside to the hotel for a few days to seek further direction.

'I was at the Feast of Tabernacles in Jerusalem,' the doctor was continuing, 'and heard a man named Steve Lightle share the most amazing vision the Lord gave him of the forthcoming exodus of Jews from the Soviet Union.'

I nearly jumped up right there. The doctor looked surprised at my excitement. But I'd been reading about this very thing in the prophets and now he told me it was happening!

I had no peace until I could get to Jerusalem and look for Steve Lightle. 'Lord,' I prayed, 'if this man is still in Israel, let me meet him. I want to know more about his vision.'

Elsa and I flew into Israel's Ben Gurion Airport two weeks later and took a taxi directly to our hotel in Jerusalem. Early the next morning we went for a walk and I pondered how we might find Steve. He had directed the European work of the Full Gospel Business Men's Fellowship International (FGBMFI). While I'd never met him personally I did hear him speak once before a crowd of 8,000 at a world convention in New Orleans. With his distinctive nose and curly grey hair it was easy to see that he himself is Jewish.

To my utter amazement, just then I saw a man who looked like Steve walking the other way across the street.

'Steve, Steve!' I shouted over the traffic. He looked our way but didn't recognize us and started to walk on.

'No, Steve, you don't know us, but we know you. I must meet you.' Elsa and I hurried across the street and caught up to him. 'We want to hear more about your vision,' I told him. He agreed to meet us the following evening for dinner.

It turned out to be an exhilarating night. Elsa and I forgot our meal as Steve shared what happened during a six-day fast in 1974. 'The power of God came in the room. It was so strong I couldn't get off the floor ... On the last day I got up and sat in a large overstuffed chair. I saw a giant screen with a multitude of Jewish faces. There were so many of them. There were hundreds of thousands of Jewish people. They were on the screen and I began to see them as they began to come together and to mill around. And I could see their faces just as I can see you across the table. And then I saw the nation they were within, and it was the Soviet Union. I could see the borders of that land. I'm sitting there watching this. This is something new. Nothing like this has ever happened to me before.

'They came together to one place and there then appeared a highway that God Himself went and built. Nobody could get on that highway except whom the Lord permitted, and these Jewish people. They got on this specially built highway and they began to walk and they began to come forth. And at the same time God raised up men with ministries as great or greater than that of Moses, who went to the authorities in the Soviet Union and proclaimed to them, "Thus saith the LORD God of Israel, 'Let My people go!'"

'And the authorities refused and wouldn't. Their hearts became hardened and they would not let the people go. And prophecies began to come, and plagues and judgment began to come against the Soviet Union until they were brought to their knees, that whole nation. And they just coughed up all these people on that highway. God built it and those Jews, hundreds of thousands of them, began to walk out.'

It sounded incredible, but Elsa and I had already begun to glimpse confirmation in the Scriptures. I knew I had more to learn and decided to remain in the country for a few weeks after Elsa returned to our children in England. Steve and his wife Judy graciously invited me to stay at their home in Ein Kerem, birthplace of John the Baptist.

Steve was exuberant, with an infectious laugh, overflowing with the joy of the Lord. As we sat around the kitchen table, instead of reading a newspaper Steve read the Word of God aloud to his family in a full voice. It was such a beautiful time, a time of learning and growing in the Word. I found that the final ingathering of the Jewish people was foretold by all the Major Prophets – appearing in over a hundred passages (see Appendix 2) – with a special emphasis on the return from 'the land of the north' (see Jeremiah 3:18, 16:15, 23:8, 31:8 and Zechariah 2:6).

Then I saw in Isaiah 49:22 God's declaration that the Gentiles would carry home the sons and daughters of the

Jewish people. I was sitting there reading and suddenly realized: **You must be part of it**. It electrified me.

Steve had only spoken of his vision publicly a handful of times in the past nine years. He would always wait on the Lord to direct him; otherwise he wouldn't take a step. But now he felt it was time to proclaim it widely, and as I watched him I realized that he had been given a message for the Church.

'One day I met a man by the name of David Pawson,' he told me. David is a well-known pastor and Bible teacher in England. 'And he looked at me and said, "God has a calling on your life. You have a prophetic role to fulfil, and Steve, you have **got** to obey God!"'

'I'll tell you,' he continued. 'In the Spirit it was as though somebody grabbed hold of me and started shaking me. It was just so powerful.'

I invited Steve to Bournemouth, the coastal town two hours south-west of London where Elsa and I lived and my business was based. As I was looking at the diary back in England, the only day that was free was Ascension Day, May 12th 1983. 'Lord,' I said, 'I think we should have a public meeting.' And somehow I felt we should take the Town Hall, one of the largest halls in town with capacity for up to 1,000 people.

So I said to my secretary, Beverley: 'Try this. If we can get the Town Hall we will take it as a sign that it is of the Lord.'

She came back into my office shortly and said, 'Yes. The Town Hall – we can have it.'

I made a provisional booking. But then I began to doubt. The Christians in our area knew little about Israel. It was unheard of at that time to fill a hall with a meeting about Jews going home. 'Lord, what am I doing?' I thought. 'We'll need 1,000 people there. I'll make a fool of myself if I bring Steve to an empty hall.'

'Lord,' I said again. 'If this is your will, then please arrange for someone to phone me with a word from Scripture as confirmation.'

I had an option that allowed me to reserve the hall for two weeks before making payment. Every day I expected something to happen, but not so. On the Sunday night before the option expired I sat in my study until midnight. I thought the phone had to ring. I was so sure we would have confirmation.

The phone didn't ring. At midnight I finally said to Elsa, 'First thing tomorrow I'll give back the Town Hall. We'll go to a church and have a low-profile meeting.'

As I was getting out of bed early the next morning the phone rang. It was a lady I didn't know well, but I respected her as a godly woman. She said, 'Gustav, I have a word from the Lord for you. I've been in prayer about the Town Hall. Would you look at Romans 10:15?'

I read it:

> 'And how shall they preach unless they are sent? As it is written:
> "How beautiful are the feet of those who preach the gospel
> of peace,
> Who bring glad tidings of good things!"'

It was a total surprise. I was amazed and relieved. Joyfully that morning I confirmed the Town Hall booking and advertised the event to the local churches.

The night before the meeting, when I came home from the office, Elsa met me at the door. 'We just had a phone call from Switzerland,' she said. Our oldest son Martin was living there with his lovely wife Debra and from the look on Elsa's face I knew something had happened.

'Martin collapsed at work,' she went on. 'He had to go to the hospital for an emergency operation.'

I had no words. It was such a shock. We were deeply troubled, not knowing what had happened. Perhaps a heart attack. Our first thought was for one of us to go at once. Steve, who was staying with us, was less perturbed. Of course it wasn't his son – but he was sure it was a spiritual attack on our meeting.

The next day we gathered in our home with others who were helping at the Town Hall that night. We fell to our knees in prayer. After some time I opened my eyes. All 25 in the room were either kneeling or flat on their faces before the Lord. It was such a mighty prayer meeting. Two words came to us:

'Your son will be healed within days – and you will light a fire for the return of the Jews that will spread through the length and breadth of the British Isles.'

Elsa and I had the peace of the Lord to stay and go on with the meeting. At the Town Hall that night we were stunned. It was filled to capacity. People had driven for hours to attend. The atmosphere was electric.

'The Lord is here with us tonight,' I said from the platform before introducing Steve. 'I wouldn't be in any other place than in the Lord's hands with God's people tonight.'

Steve came and related his vision as we had first heard it in Jerusalem. Then he paused.

'I might say right now, if anybody wants to leave, you're perfectly welcome to leave at this moment. If you don't, you're going to be just as responsible for what you're going to hear as I am.'

Five seconds passed. You could have heard a pin drop. Nobody moved.

'This, to my knowledge, is the first time this message has been publicly shared within the UK. **This will go through your whole nation** so that no one will ever be able to say, "Well, that was a freak accident of history." Everybody shall know what the Lord God is going to do.'

'I want to read to you one representative set of Scriptures out of Jeremiah 23,' Steve continued. Each person had received at the door a list of many of the great ingathering Scriptures: Deuteronomy 30; Isaiah 11, 35, 43; Jeremiah 3, 16, 23, 30, 31; Ezekiel 36–39; Zephaniah 3. 'Let's understand something of what God wants to do in the last days. Why is it so prophetic for us here tonight? Why are the Jews of the Soviet Union so prophetic to God in the last days? Why is God beginning to place them on the hearts of believers around the whole world? And not only believers, but now I'm meeting Jewish people and God has spoken to their hearts what He's going to do with the Jews of the Soviet Union.

> *"'But I will gather the remnant of My flock out of all countries where I have driven them, and bring them back to their folds; and they shall be fruitful and increase. I will set up shepherds over them who will feed them; and they shall fear no more, nor be dismayed, nor shall they be lacking," says the LORD.*
>
> *"Behold, the days are coming," says the LORD,*
> *"That I will raise to David a Branch of righteousness;*
> *A King shall reign and prosper,*
> *And execute judgment and righteousness in the earth.*
> *In His days Judah will be saved,*
> *And Israel will dwell safely;*
> *Now this is His name by which He will be called:*
> *THE LORD OUR RIGHTEOUSNESS.'"*
>
> Jeremiah 23:3–6

'What is the prophet telling us?' Steve continued. 'He's saying, "Listen. There is a day coming in the history of the world – God is going to gather His ancient people, the Jewish people, back from the four corners of the earth. And when they are gathered back and when they are returned to the land, **then** I shall raise up the righteous Branch." And He shall come forth, not as a lamb led to the slaughter, but He shall come as the King of kings, He shall come as the Lord of lords.

'And brothers and sisters, **that** is the second coming of the Lord Jesus, and when He comes all the Jewish people of the world, from all the countries to which He's scattered them, shall be back in Israel. He's not coming back to a land that's vacant of His ancient people. He's coming back and it's going to be full of the ancient people of God. For it will be the fulfilment of the prophecy of Zechariah chapter 12 verse 10: *"And they shall behold Him whom they pierced."* And the weeping that's going to come – but I'll tell you then it'll be turned to tears of joy. You're going to see an explosion that only God can orchestrate by His Holy Spirit.

'Now how can I make such a bold statement as that? God does things prophetically. Before Jesus came there was one called John the Baptist that went forth with a voice crying in the wilderness: *"Prepare ye the way of the Lord."* He was the prophetic preparation for the Messiah to come. And when Jesus comes again He will have a prophetic preparation and it is the return of the Jews from around the world.

'But it begins in a specific nation. How do we know? Let's go on to verse 7: *"'Therefore...'"* It is a conjunction. It relates back to these prior verses.

> *"'Therefore, behold, the days are coming," says the* LORD, *"that they shall no longer say, 'As the* LORD *lives who brought up the children of Israel from the land of Egypt,' but, 'As the* LORD *lives who brought up and led the descendants of the house of Israel from the north country and from all the countries where I had driven them.' And they shall dwell in their own land.'"*
>
> Jeremiah 23:7-8

'There is only one nation to the north of Israel today that has any sizable number of Jews in it. That is the Soviet Union, with 2.1 million.

'God is going to give an opportunity to the nations of the world to bless His people, no matter what nation they're in, and it is to help them return to Israel. That's what we're doing here tonight. If your heart is open to hear the truth of God, take these verses, go to your prayer closet, and say, "God, is this true?"'

None of us were the same after the message of that night. Many in the audience had never heard what the Bible says about the return of the Jews. 'It was an eye-opener to have those Scriptures pointed out,' one woman said. 'I must have read them without understanding.' Israel just wasn't a topic in our churches. We'd always thought of the passages in the Bible about Israel only as teaching illustrations for application in our own lives.

The promised fire was lit – and when Elsa flew out the next day to Switzerland she found our son was indeed already recovering from what doctors said was a collapsed lung.

So Steve and I teamed up and travelled together to bring this message to the Church in the UK. I recall those days so well. 'It's time that somebody began to tell the leadership of the Soviet Union what the word of the Lord says,' Steve declared everywhere we went. 'Either they bow their knee to God, or God is going to judge them. One or the other.' Following a news conference at the Finnish parliament the BBC World Service broadcast the challenge across the globe. One of the major Soviet newspapers mocked it under the headline 'God Brings Russia to its Knees.'

Even the believers would look at us with big eyes in these meetings and think we were funny guys. It seemed impossible to believe in 1983 that communism would fall and the Jews be released; it was the height of the Cold War. The Soviet Union was at the peak of its military power and world influence, expanding its empire into places like Afghanistan, Nicaragua, and Angola. A vigorous Yuri Andropov, who headed the KGB for 15 years and directed the harassment and imprisonment of Jews wishing to emigrate, had taken the reins of power when Leonid Brezhnev died just six months before the Town Hall meeting.

None of us realized it but the wheels of judgment had already started to turn. From 1979 on the Soviet grain harvests were so disastrous the authorities simply stopped reporting the statistics. Heavy rains spoiled the planting; withering heat stunted the growing season; then heavy rains returned at harvest time to flatten crops and leave those still standing sodden. In Moscow, Marxist historian Roy Medvedev, in an article headlined 'Why the Russians Can't Grow Grain', reached the conclusion that 'in agriculture, 50% depends on God.'

The unthinkable was happening: a modern industrialized superpower faced famine. A call went out to the public to conserve food. To prevent starvation the Soviet leadership was forced to spend nearly half of its annual hard currency earnings on food imports – just as there was a sharp rise in military spending by the United States under Ronald Reagan. Squeezed from both sides, the Soviet Union was approaching bankruptcy.

Then one morning 15 months after Andropov took power Moscow awoke to funereal music on the radio. After hours of speculation the world was told: Andropov – despite recent Kremlin assurances of his good health – was dead. He was succeeded by Konstantin Chernenko, aged 72, but was still a year younger than his counterpart, Reagan.

Thirteen months later classical music returned to the radio in Moscow in place of a comedy programme. The next afternoon came the stunning news that Chernenko, too, was dead. Brezhnev, Andropov, and Chernenko, all gone in less than two-and-a-half years. Until then the average tenure of a General Secretary had been nearly 20 years! The deaths of the two shortest-serving rulers in Soviet history cleared the way for the meteoric rise of a younger, lesser-known man named Mikhail Gorbachev.

At the time fewer than 100 Jews a month were then allowed to emigrate. Over 360,000 who had dared to apply were refused, even as the Communist Party told the world 'all who want to leave have already gone'. Anatoly Sharansky, leader of the emigration movement, was in his seventh year in a labour camp for 'treason and anti-Soviet agitation'.

A select group of intercessors, including Steve, Johannes and Kjell Sjoberg, arrived a month after Gorbachev took power and travelled to all the major Jewish centres in the Soviet Union. In each place they encircled at least one of the many giant statues of Lenin, praying and proclaiming that this idol would fall. They sought out traffic points – airports, harbours and railway stations – and prayed that the Lord would open them up for sending Jews back to Israel. At the Ukrainian Black Sea port of Odessa they fanned out across the massive Potemkin steps leading from the city down to the port, and went slowly down the steps praying. At the bottom they turned and went back up doing the same – nearly bumping into their KGB tails.

Such on-site spiritual warfare was at the time rather unusual. Back at their hotel over coffee the men laughed and admitted they felt foolish for what they were doing. 'What do we hope to accomplish by this?' asked Johannes, hesitantly. Back home others in his church shared his scepticism.

And, in fact, during his first nine months as general secretary Gorbachev proved just as obstinate toward the Jews as his predecessors. He told French television interviewers that Jews enjoyed more 'political and other rights' in the USSR than in any other country, and trotted out the party line that only those who 'know state secrets' were prevented from leaving. Challenged about Anatoly Sharansky, Gorbachev declared that he had 'breached our laws and was sentenced by court for that'.

At the end of the year Steve and Johannes returned to the USSR, this time with a team of 13 other intercessors from France, Sweden, Finland, the USA and Germany. Their mission: to proclaim judgment on the pharaoh who still refused to let God's people go. By resisting God's timing for fulfilment of His word, they believed the Soviet Union had entered on a collision course with the Almighty Himself and had to be broken. 'We have a feeling God is putting an end to this whole thing,' Johannes said. The team prepared with three days of prayer and fasting in Finland, taking the theme from Jeremiah 51 of judgment and devastation coming on the land.

On the bitter cold afternoon of December 31 they proclaimed outside Gorbachev's office in Moscow the words Samuel once spoke to Saul: *'Because you have rejected the word of the* LORD, *He has rejected you as king. The* LORD *has torn the kingdom from you today.'*

The intercessors then crossed Red Square, walking along the fortress walls of the Kremlin and praying in the Spirit. A Finnish pastor pointed to the top of a tower where a great red star was illuminated against the darkening afternoon sky.

'What does that mean?' he asked the group.

'It's a symbol of man and the strength of man,' said a Swedish member who specialized in occult and New Age research. 'The communist system represents trust in man. The Soviets worship scientific achievement. But Jeremiah 17:5 says, *"Cursed is the man who trusts in man and makes flesh his strength."'*

The men continued to walk and pray. 'I have a sense of that star falling down,' one said after a few minutes, the others nodding in agreement. 'And it will happen very soon.'

That night the group came together at their hotel. 'Listen to what it says in Revelation 8!' one of the team exclaimed, opening his Bible: 'A star falling from heaven. This is what we were praying about today.'

At midnight the group went down to the Moscow river beside the Kremlin and, following the instructions in Jeremiah 51:59–64 to an intercessor, took a Bible marked with passages of judgment, tied it to a large stone, and threw it through the thin ice covering the river. 'Thus the Soviet Union shall sink and not rise from the catastrophe that I will bring upon her,' they declared in the name of the LORD.

'Everything seemed so crazy,' one of the men said afterwards, 'impossible to the human mind. But we knew God was in it.'

Four months later came the event that sent shock waves through the Soviet Union and the world: the explosion and uncontrolled fire at the Chernobyl nuclear reactor in the Ukraine. The accident emitted as much long-term radiation into the world's air, topsoil, and water as all nuclear tests and bombs yet exploded. Local and regional Communist Party officials attempted to cover up what was happening, sending their own children away while ordering others to march in May Day celebrations even as a lethal radioactive cloud hung over the region.

Thousands suffered from headaches, coughing and spitting blood. Only when the cloud rained down contamination on Poland, the Scandinavian countries and beyond did the story begin to leak out. Eventually hundreds of thousands of residents were permanently evacuated from the Chernobyl region – too late. Many had been exposed to enough radiation to kill them over the coming years, as were an unknown number of the 600,000 workers sent in for the massive clean-up attempt. When the full truth came out it tore the mask from the face of the communist leadership and more than any other factor caused the people to lose faith in the Soviet system.

Left contaminated was a huge swathe of the Soviet Union's premier farming region and water supply. In a failing effort to prevent contamination of the groundwater, deep wells were sunk around Chernobyl and airplanes treated the clouds above to limit rainfall. Kiev, the Soviet Union's third largest city just over 100 kilometres to the south, was forced to develop an alternative water supply. Because of lake contamination limits were put on the consumption of sweet water fish in Finland and increased radiation was detected in rainwater as far away as the east coast of the United States.

Then within a few months of the disaster came a startling realization, as reported on the front page of *The New York Times* in a July 26th 1986 dispatch from Moscow:

'A prominent Russian writer recently produced a tattered old Bible and with a practised hand turned to Revelation. 'Listen,' he said, 'this is incredible':

'And the third angel sounded, and there fell a great star from heaven, burning as it were a lamp, and it fell upon the third part of the rivers and upon the fountains of waters; and the name of the star is called wormwood: and the third part of the waters became wormwood; and many men died of the waters, because they were made bitter.'

In a dictionary he showed that the Ukrainian word for wormwood, a bitter wild herb used as a tonic in rural Russia is chernobyl.

The writer, an atheist, was hardly alone in pointing out the apocalyptic reference to the star called chernobyl. The discovery had spread across the Soviet land with uncanny speed.'

None but God knows the connection between the Revelation passage and Chernobyl, between the intercession of the Church and the disaster that came upon the Soviet Union. But of the significance of Chernobyl there is no question. 'It shook us greatly,' Gorbachev said, looking back years later. 'It was a turning point.' *Glasnost* (openness) would be the result, coupled with the *perestroika* (restructuring), which sought to deal with the Soviet Union's ongoing economic crisis.

The iron gates that held the Jewish people were starting to shake. And we remembered Steve's words at the Town Hall: 'Nobody will ever be able to say, "Well, that was a freak accident of history." No!'

CHAPTER 2

The Summons

'This is what the Sovereign LORD says:

"See, I will beckon to the Gentiles,
I will lift up My banner to the peoples;
They will bring your sons in their arms
And carry your daughters on their shoulders."'

Isaiah 49:22 – NIV

During the following years the intercessory prayer conference in Jerusalem became an annual event and I took care of the practical arrangements. Eventually I found myself praying 'Lord, have I served enough tables?' I knew He had promoted the deacons of old to spiritual works as well. 'I just don't want to be a Stephen, Lord!'

I will never forget what happened when I sat across a hotel breakfast table in Jerusalem from Bill Styles, a Baptist minister who was working as a travel agent in Israel. He looked at me intently and said, 'I had a dream two months ago. And in this dream I was standing in a huge terminal surrounded by many people, old and young, poorly-dressed, with their luggage at their sides. I realized they were Jews. Nobody seemed to know what to do. Then I noticed a man came in dressed in a business suit. He had white hair and was carrying a briefcase. He knew what to do.

'And the Lord spoke to me that I would help this man in bringing Jewish people home from the ends of the earth. As soon as I saw you this morning I recognized you. I can tell you, it was you I saw in the dream.'

It was as if the Lord would hit me over my head and ask me, 'How many times do I have to tell you? One day you will help the Jews from the land of the north to go home.'

Waiting for things has never been my strength, but in a way I knew the vision was for the appointed time. The Lord began to prepare me by gently weaning me from the business I'd built up over the years since coming to England from Switzerland.

As Elsa will testify, at one time I had been married to my work. I brought in overseas visitors and opened language schools for them in Oxford, Cambridge, London, Torquay and Bournemouth, as well as travel offices in a number of cities around Britain. My business expanded and I eventually opened offices in Switzerland, Japan and the US, with representatives in many other countries. As the market leader in incoming tourism I received the Queen's Award to Industry and was invited to Buckingham Palace. My secret ambition was to be knighted one day.

All this changed on a wet and misty Sunday in the autumn of 1979 when Elsa, our four children and I dressed up and trooped off to church, a lifelong ritual in keeping with my upbringing. There was a new minister at the Winton Methodist Church and on this morning I was surprised to see him open the pulpit to a group of ordinary lay people. They stood at the front of the old stone church and shared simply from their own lives how God had touched them.

It was as if I heard it for the first time. I called myself a Christian and could be found warming the same pew each Sunday. But the other six days of the week I lived the way I wanted. Now I was challenged to hear that only by repentance could I be a child of God.

When they finished speaking they asked for those who would yield their lives to come forward, something that had never happened before in all my years at the church. It was embarrassing – I was the church treasurer – but somehow I knew that I had to get up from my pew. I went down the aisle, past the congregation and knelt at the communion rail at the foot of a big wooden cross. Tears ran down my cheeks. At the age of 50 I became a follower of Jesus.

I was too overwhelmed to speak when I returned to where Elsa was sitting and felt her hand take mine. I could see she was stunned and thrilled. She had prayed for this for years.

Alone in my study that night I picked up the Living Bible, which fell open to the story of the prodigal son in Luke 15. One phrase stood out as though illuminated:

> '"This son of mine was dead and has returned to life. He was lost and is found." So the party began.'

I sensed that my new life would bring joy and fulfilment, which, despite my worldly success, I had not yet experienced. My business had done so well over many years, but it started to crumble over the following months. It was the time of an oil crisis, high inflation and high interest rates. Travel came almost to a standstill and I found I had over-expanded the work. After much agonizing I had to lay off 80 of my permanent staff of 220. It really burdened me. I spoke to each man and woman myself and lifted them up in prayer.

Still the company went down. Many days I sat at my desk calculating how many days and weeks remained before I had to put the whole business into liquidation. My life's work was coming to the abyss – all would collapse. I was proud of my achievements. All my life I'd been building up. But now there was nothing I could do. I was just helpless, fighting against a brick wall.

On my 51st birthday I tried something I'd never done before. I asked the Lord to give me a word. Elsa and I were starting each day with a reading from a book of Scripture texts called *Daily Watchwords*, born out of a powerful visitation of the Holy Spirit in 1727 to a community of persecuted Moravian believers who had taken refuge in the village of Herrnhut, Germany. Brethren would go from house to house each morning bringing the 'watchword' for the day as a guide to meditation. Eventually the passages for each year were chosen by lot and published in advance. We were now reading from the 250th edition.

That morning's reading was Jesus speaking to Martha:

> *'You are worried and troubled about many things. But one thing is needed.'*

'Yes, Lord,' I confessed, 'I am troubled about the business, the staff, the debts.'

I understood I should release my problems to Him. He was well able to deal with them. 'Lord, give me the chance,' I told Him. 'I want to go before you; I want to really just have this intimate relationship with you. But you must help me.'

I wanted to be entirely sure that this word was for me. Perhaps I wasn't quite ready. In the evening I turned to my American prayer diary – and found exactly the same word for that day. That hit me. It had never happened in all the time we were reading both prayer diaries. I knew God had spoken. I realized He was testing me, so over a period of time I came to the point of saying, 'Lord, this is your business. I hand it over completely to you. You can do whatever you want with it.'

It took some time to work out this surrender. One can say it – but saying and doing are often two different things.

One morning as we were under severe financial pressure I met with an Englishwoman who was my agent in Turkey. She owed me a substantial sum.

'I need this money!' I told her, rapping my fist on the desk to emphasize each word.

'Mr Scheller, I can't meet my obligations,' she told me. She was desperate. Suddenly I knew I had to help **her**. She walked out at the end of the meeting with £1,000.

'I'm going a bit funny,' I told Elsa that night. 'At a time when we can't pay bills and salaries I'm giving cash away.'

We turned then to our evening reading from Deuteronomy 15:

> *'You shall surely give to* [your poor brother], *and your heart should not be grieved when you give to him, because for this thing the* LORD *your God will bless you in all your works and in all to which you put your hand.'*
>
> Deuteronomy 15:10

We had a praise party knowing that I had done the right thing. I had built in Bournemouth, with the help of a substantial bank loan, a four-storey office block as well as a school with good administrative facilities. I knew that if I could sell one of these buildings I would gain breathing space and the business could return to profitability. But I soon realized that I was not the only one trying to sell an office block; other companies were also in trouble and trying to do the same.

Bournemouth is one of the central points in southern England to coordinate bus traffic and a modern administrative block had been built for this purpose. This building caught fire and became unusable. Almost overnight new facilities were needed to continue the work. They took over my building. My business was saved from liquidation.

At the same time it was as if the Lord opened the tap and business began to flow freely. I can't explain how it happened, but what looked a desperate situation, as weeks went by, turned into a very handsome profit picture. In that year I made more profit than in any other. But the business now truly belonged to the Lord. I realized that I depend on Him and that not all was due to my own good efforts.

After some years I had an attractive takeover offer for my language schools and the Lord reminded me that I had released the business to Him. Feeling loyalty to my staff, I told the senior people. They offered a management buyout instead, which I gratefully accepted.

I was still left with the travel company, but on its own – without the administrative support from the school staff – it began to lose money. I became anxious. We needed the Lord's direction to show a way of escape. I didn't see a way to put it up for sale, as it was a losing venture.

Elsa and I started a 'Daniel fast' for three weeks, going without meat and sweets as Daniel and companions had once done in Babylon. Nothing happened. We continued with a full fast for a few days.

Then in the post at home one morning came a very official-looking letter labelled 'Strictly Private'. I picked it up off the floor, intrigued, took it to the breakfast table and opened it first. It was from a consultant who had instructions from a major business house to acquire a travel company. Even though I had given no public indication that I wanted to sell, he had analysed the market and concluded that our company was exactly what they wanted.

I chuckled. Who wants to buy a company that is losing money? 'The Lord has funny ways of dealing with our problems,' I said to Elsa.

A few weeks later I went to London to meet the chairman and finance director. These were top guys in a multi-million pound organization. It was not a good meeting. Somehow I felt we were not speaking the same language. I concluded there would be no deal.

But to my surprise a few days later the chairman drove down to see me at my office in Bournemouth. Above the conference table was a small plaque stating 'Jesus Christ is Lord'. The chairman looked at this and told me, 'I am a Catholic. I studied two years for the priesthood, but realized it was not my calling.'

I just listened, but it established a relationship that was not there before. A mutual trust transpired. 'Make us an offer, including staff details,' he said before leaving. I put one carefully together and sent it off, and a few days later two of his auditors turned up to inspect our books. My heart sank. They would soon realize it was not a profitable venture.

It didn't take long – a phone call came inviting me to the head office. There the chairman said that he wanted to buy the company exactly on the conditions I had submitted! I'll never forget that afternoon when the finance director handed me a letter of intent for the purchase of the company. He stood and just laughed and laughed, and finally said, 'Mr Scheller, I have no clue why we should buy your company.' I laughed too, all the way back to Bournemouth – free now for the call the Lord had given me years before.

Then came the miracle we had prayed and worked for through the years. As part of Gorbachev's reforms sweeping the Soviet Union, in December 1989 the gates swung open and the Jewish people were free to leave. Nearly 200,000 rushed out to Israel over the next 13 months. On the eve of our January 1991 prayer conference in Jerusalem a record 35,295 repatriates arrived in one month.

But other events were gripping the attention of the world. Iraqi dictator Saddam Hussein had invaded Kuwait and was rapidly approaching confrontation with a US-led coalition. If attacked he threatened to 'burn up half of Israel' – understood as a reference to Iraqi missiles capable of reaching Israel with chemical warheads.

The first day of the prayer conference turned out to be the deadline for Iraq to withdraw. Governments warned their citizens to stay out of the region. Most foreign airlines cancelled their flights in and out of Israel, and almost all tourists abandoned their plans to be in the country at the time. But 120 totally committed Christians from 24 nations turned up at the Holyland Hotel, taking their theme from the biblical call to '*stand in the gap before Me for the land*'.

This group had been sifted. There were many late cancellations, but these were outnumbered by last-minute bookings. All knew it could cost their lives. Some had fought to come to Israel against the counsel of family and government. These were real intercessors, wanting to stand with those they prayed for.

As the threat of a massive attack loomed over us the first night we gathered and sang the old hymn 'Great is Thy Faithfulness'. A great strength and peace came over the group and we were absolutely secure in God's hand. We all felt it a privilege and a joy to be in the land at a time like this.

Elsa and I had hardly fallen asleep that night when the telephone jangled by the bedside in our room. The traveller's alarm clock showed 2:15 a.m. Even before picking up the phone I knew: the war had started.

For a moment I was gripped by a sudden burden for the innocent Iraqis who would suffer while Saddam was hidden safely away. Then fully awake I sat up in bed and began making wake-up calls of my own. Within quarter of an hour the long carpeted corridors filled with quietly talking people. The allied bombardment of Baghdad had begun. 'How will Iraq respond?' was the question I heard on many lips.

Our answer came at the same hour the next night. I was awakened to the ghostly drone of air raid sirens rising, holding a pitch and then slowly receding. American satellites had detected the launching of Iraqi Scud missiles toward Israel – they would land in two minutes.

Elsa and I were sleeping in tracksuits. We had only to grab the cardboard cartons holding our gas masks and rush to the sealed room on our floor, protected against chemical attack by plastic sheeting taped over the windows and insulation around the door. Others joined us, moving quickly but without panic.

In the room I took off my spectacles to put on the gas mask, pulling the elastic straps snugly behind my head. I glanced around the room and couldn't help thinking we looked almost more like dogs than humans. We waited for news on the radio of what was happening, each rubbery breath an effort. We couldn't speak to each other but certainly did speak to the Lord.

Nearly two hours passed before a woman's voice came on the radio: 'All residents of Israel may remove gas masks and depart from sealed rooms.'

A spirit of joy erupted and we just began praising the Lord. We heard that missiles with conventional warheads had damaged homes in Tel Aviv and Haifa, but there were no deaths or serious injuries. Messages of encouragement began to come in from believers around the world who were watching these events on television.

The night-time alarms continued throughout the week. It was an emotionally charged time. I awoke one night when I heard a noise and jumped out of bed.

'*Schatz*,' I cried to Elsa, using our Swiss German term of endearment. 'Can't you hear the siren going?'

She lifted her head from the pillow and cocked an ear. 'No, I don't hear anything.'

Irritated, I opened the window and stuck my head out. I heard only a passing truck.

'Sorry, *schatz*, I was wrong.' It was an exercise we repeated more than once during the week, interspersed with half a dozen real attacks, which we waited out in the sealed rooms.

But even as the missile attacks continued I had the persistent feeling that I was in the right place. There was no anxiety in me or in the group. We knew we were in God's hands. It was the best conference I ever coordinated. There was a unity you only reach at a time of crisis. We moved as an army under a powerful anointing of the Holy Spirit.

We prayed that through the war God would prepare the way for the fulfilment of two biblically-based promises: to bring the gospel to the Muslim world and bring the children of Israel back to their Promised Land. Many think intercession in these cases is something done only on our knees. But as the conference went on I had an overwhelming sense that God wanted us also to take action: **Now you can begin helping My people to go home**.

I knew Johannes, spiritual leader of the conference, well enough to predict his reaction. 'This is silly,' he would think. 'We're sitting in the basement with gas masks on, talking about bringing Jews under the bombardment of Saddam Hussein.' Johannes and I were usually the most practically minded of the conference organizers. But somehow I had to go ahead.

I went to Johannes. 'I have the distinct impression,' I told him, 'that now is the time the Lord wants us to help the Jews come home from the land of the north.'

To my amazement, Johannes nodded in agreement. 'Yes – yes, Gustav, I believe this is of the Lord.' We were both so surprised! It was just like God.

Another barrage of missiles landed in Israel at 7:00 a.m. Shabbat morning. That evening I went before the 120 and shared my impression. To my further amazement, they too unanimously sensed this was a sovereign move of God. They gave an offering for the exodus of Soviet Jewry. With two men I counted it afterwards – and this little group had given $30,000.

We all rejoiced at the confirmation of what God was saying. But if I'd known at the time how things would unfold from there I probably would have gone into hiding.

CHAPTER 3

First Flights

'Who are these who fly like a cloud,
And like doves to their roosts?'
Isaiah 60:8

'I don't think the prophet Isaiah ever saw an airplane,' Steve quipped. 'The best way he could describe it was a cloud with wings.' At 4:40 a.m. on a Thursday morning four months after the prayer conference, we stood with a small crowd of supporters on the tarmac at Israel's Ben Gurion airport. The sky was just lightening in the east as the door of a white and blue El Al plane swung open and the first of 250 *olim* (pronounced oh-leem – new immigrants; literally 'those going up' to Israel) came down the stairs for their first step on Israeli soil. The first person to leave the aircraft was a lady of 86 in a ragged dress carrying a small red plastic bowl that contained all her worldly possessions. She wept as she was presented with roses, chocolates and a Bible – things she had never been able to enjoy.

We saw small children, some clutching dolls and one a small puppy. There were old folks who could hardly make their way down the steps. Some were well dressed, others obviously very poor.

A man went to his hands and knees and kissed the tarmac. The crowd cheered and waved Israeli flags. There was so much excitement. Some *olim* were laughing, some singing, others weeping and spontaneously embracing each other. We felt like Peter at Pentecost: *'This is that which was spoken by the prophet.'* It was an awesome experience to see them coming for the first time. All that we had talked and prayed about through the 1980s we now saw happening with our own eyes.

With the collection from the prayer conference I had turned to the Jewish Agency, the body which until that time had organized all *aliyah* (all-lee-ya – immigration, 'going up' to Israel), to see how we could sponsor a flight. We had nothing at the time. There was the prayer conference mailing list of a few hundred names and a group of about 60–80 believers who would turn out for an evening meeting in Bournemouth. We met in a basement room of a building which Elsa and I called Ebenezer House, after Samuel's testimony in 1 Samuel 7:12 that, *'Thus far the* LORD *has helped us.'*

We sent out simple material explaining what we felt we had to do, called it Operation Exodus and set up the Ebenezer Emergency Fund to administer it. I was surprised to get quite a lot of mail in return from people I'd never heard of. But they were so stirred. They knew the Bible and understood the time for the return of God's chosen people had come. One family with three young children wrote to me, 'We're not going on holiday this year. It's more important for a Jewish family to go home.' I had never experienced this kind of giving in my life. I sat behind my desk and just wept when I saw how my brothers and sisters were giving.

I got letters daily from Christians who spoke of the love they had for the Jewish people. They wrote, 'Dear Gustav, thank you so much that we can send you this money for a ticket.' It really baffled me. I would read that and think, 'If I gave someone money I would hope they would write a letter to thank me!'

Many of the gifts came from those who had hardly any money. Three blind ladies met in the north of England and saved together to sponsor a passenger. An invalid lady in her sixties living on a pension sent us a letter every month with £2.

She took this out of her pension of £49. These really had to be wise keepers of their money. It reminded me more than once of the widow's mite in Luke 21.

Gifts came from Christians in nearly 30 nations. I was astounded at what was happening. A group of about 30 Korean ladies wrote to us. They had no money to give but were praying for us and would contact us later. Their next letter included a cheque for $7,500. 'We decided not only to pray,' they wrote, 'but to ask for overtime pay from our jobs – and every penny we received over 30 days went to help the Jewish people home.'

An American couple had started a church in Mexico that grew to 22 congregations. They stood with Israel and God blessed their ministry. 'As I shared the return of the Jews with the poorest of my congregations – people who live in huts with corrugated metal covers as roofs – they decided they wanted to pay for a ticket,' the pastor told me. 'For them even a dollar is a fortune. But they gathered the money together to pay for it.'

The other side that deeply thrilled me was the giving attitude of the Jewish people themselves. The day after our flight arrived the Israeli government launched an operation to rescue more than 14,000 black Ethiopian Jews, after receiving news of bitter battles between the Ethiopian government and rebels. Forty flights came thundering in during a massive airlift called Operation Solomon. Five babies were born aboard the aircraft!

Elsa and I visited the Diplomat Hotel in Jerusalem, which the government commandeered and filled with 1,200 of the new arrivals. They had brought no luggage with them, just the clothes they were wearing, the women in their traditional robes. When news of this broke the Jerusalemites filled their cars with clothes, food, medicine, and toys and drove up. Tears came to my eyes when I saw how they welcomed their brothers and sisters. After six hours the police had to barricade the roads leading to the hotel, as they were unable to accept any more aid. Romans 11:11 says we should make the Jews jealous; often they have made me jealous.

Elsa and I then went to Budapest to see the Jewish Agency transit camp from which the *olim* had embarked on our flight. The Soviet Union allowed no direct flights to Israel, so all repatriates were first routed through the Eastern European cities of Budapest, Bucharest, or Warsaw. 'Three days ago we had a young girl who was dying of cancer,' the camp director told us. 'She only had a few days to live. After talking it over, we decided she should die in her true homeland.' They found a doctor and nurse and flew her to Israel.

Early the next morning we went with the Agency team to the central train station in Budapest. As we drove along one of them drew our attention to the river Danube. 'During the Holocaust,' he said quietly, 'members of my family were pushed in and drowned here.' At the train station we learned that Jews were once packed into cattle cars there and sent to the death camp at Auschwitz. Now trains were coming in with *olim* from the Soviet Union.

We walked into the station past a young man kneeling on the ground fiddling with his rucksack and my escort gave me a little nudge. Instantly I knew this was Israeli security. As we walked around the station I gradually realized there were about half a dozen men in different places. One was reading the paper, but he wasn't really reading; he was watching the movement in the station. There were three trains coming in that day at different hours and the Russian trains don't run on Swiss time. Often these men had to wait for hours and hours. Elsa and I were deeply impressed by the commitment and sacrifice of the Israeli team.

We went on to sponsor a second and then a third Jewish Agency flight from Budapest, bringing a total of 720 *olim*. But by the time of our third flight in May I'd begun to get letters from believers reminding me that Isaiah's remarkable vision of Jews returning by air continued with:

'The ships of Tarshish will come first,
to bring your sons from afar,
their silver and their gold with them.'

Isaiah 60:9

'Gustav, what about a ship?' they wrote.

I didn't want to hear about a ship. I knew nothing about ships. It is so much easier to write about ships than to do it. I said, 'Lord, if that is of you I must know from you.'

Early in June 1991 I was talking with a prayer partner in my office and I brought up all my excuses. 'Listen,' I said. 'This is mission impossible. We would need permits from the Israelis, from the Soviets, from the port authorities. We would need to establish a transit camp to sleep and feed hundreds of people. It is already difficult just to feed one family. We would have to provide security, we would need a big passenger ship and we would need an awful lot of money.'

'But,' I said, taking my friend to see a copper plate which had hung on my office wall for years, 'I serve a great God. Look, the Scripture inscribed here says, *"For with God all things are possible"* (Mark 10:27).' As I spoke this out suddenly for the first time I saw there was the image of a ship above the words. Somehow I'd never noticed it before.

It was as if the Lord Himself put His hand on my head and said, 'For with Me a ship is possible.' I broke down and wept. All doubt vanished.

Almost immediately I left for Jerusalem, full of joy. I'd learned through the years that when the Lord speaks I run. If I wait then doubts come. He wants us to trust Him, even if we think it's absolutely crazy. His ways are so much higher than ours.

I went alone to the big stone headquarters of the Jewish Agency. I hoped they would cooperate with us in some way: perhaps release *olim* from their network to travel on a ship. I climbed the staircase to the second floor executive corridor, walked past the photos of the century's great Zionists and came to an office where two senior officials were waiting for me.

I thanked them for the good cooperation we'd enjoyed in working on the flights. 'Now the time has come to take this a step further,' I said, picking up my Bible.

'This is **your** Bible,' I told them, 'the word of the living God. And the prophet Isaiah says here that your people will return by air **and** by ships. We'd like to work with you on opening a sea route to Israel.'

The two looked at each other and smiled. They were still gracious – we had paid for flights and there was a good chance we would continue to do so – but there certainly wasn't the same interest in helping with a ship.

They gave a word of caution to dampen my enthusiasm. 'Others have tried and failed. There hasn't been a direct route from the Soviet Union – for flights or sailings – since the establishment of the state.'

We shook hands and I walked back down the corridor of power, down the staircase and out into the hot summer sun.

'They think it's a crazy idea that will fizzle out and I will come to my senses,' I mused.

I shared their reaction with Elsa afterwards. 'They are happy to accept our financial contributions, but hadn't counted on us wanting hands-on involvement.'

'They're so strong, so set in themselves,' she said. 'It must seem amusing for nobodies like us from the outside to come and tell them how to bring Jews home.'

Everywhere I turned I wasn't well received. There were no takers willing to come alongside. Doors were slammed in my face one after the other. Even among Christians in Jerusalem I didn't initially find any great enthusiasm for this project. I was a bit shaken. Maybe it was an illusion to think that they would all stand ready to welcome me.

For three days in my Jerusalem apartment the Lord made

me withdraw from the outside world, praying, fasting, seeking His face. I was quite miserable. On one side I was pregnant with a ship. There was no question about it. But I didn't see any breakthrough, and unlike those who say fasting does them good, I get headaches. I was on the floor before the Lord. It was a time when the refining fire of the Holy Spirit was working in my own life and rarely have I felt so inadequate for my task as I did during these days. More than ever I could sympathize with Jonah who wanted to run away from his task.

I was flat on my face when in walked Ted Walker, a brother with a pure heart who always encourages me. 'I don't know where to turn any more,' I told him. We cried out together to the Lord. It was a prayer of desperation, a time when all my own good ideas had to die. Every door had been closed. It seemed the battle was lost. 'Lord,' I said, 'this is your work, not mine.'

That's when God takes us by the hand and says 'Now child, I'll show you My way.' He does it in a way that we know it has been of His Spirit and not of the flesh.

The phone rang in the apartment. It was a sympathetic official from the Jewish Agency. 'Would you be able to meet a man named David at the Hilton Hotel in Zurich in two days?' He gave no further details, not even the man's surname. He spoke in such secretive terms that I thought it could be a Mossad man I would meet. I sensed it was not a time to ask questions – it was time to act.

I flew to Zurich. I'd agreed to meet this man in the hotel lobby. I walked in ahead of the scheduled time. There were a number of people milling about, but my eyes were drawn to a man sitting in the far corner and instantly I knew it was my contact. He turned out to be an Israeli businessman who wanted a ship for import/export business with the Soviet Union.

We talked about a partnership for some time, so much so that David missed his plane to Geneva. Another Israeli businessman turned up and gave him a lift in his private jet, but the next day David was forced to return to Zurich to find a seat on a flight to Tel Aviv. He was astonished to find himself sitting directly behind me on the plane. 'There are certain things happening here that are not natural!' he exclaimed. We resumed our discussions.

David represented a powerful business consortium and back in Israel doors suddenly flew open at every level. Talks began with shipping companies and port authorities. We gained strong support in the Knesset (Israeli parliament) from Michael Kleiner, chairman of the *aliyah* committee. 'I will be your umbrella,' he told me. 'I myself came to Israel by ship back in 1951.' He wrote to us that he was 'deeply touched by the generous donations from Christians around the world'. To help us negotiate with the government of the Soviet Union we also won the cooperation of the prime minister's Liaison Bureau, which had maintained relations with Soviet Jewry during the years this was officially forbidden.

'We have a vision to carry 25,000 Jews back to their homeland,' I had the boldness to tell these government officials. I estimated it would require a budget of $10,000,000 - $12,000,000. All the gold and silver belongs to my heavenly Father and my faith was growing that He would see that all the funds needed were available on time.

From the beginning we focused on the port of Odessa as the best-situated gateway from the Soviet Union. It would allow for a direct sea route, without the crossing of any international borders. In his vision Steve had seen Jewish people coming out across Europe and boarding ships in Holland, and some believers along this route had made preparations. Both Steve and I felt this route might be used during a later and greater stage of the exodus – but with the flights and now the shipping I was obedient to what the Lord was showing me.

The time had come to go to the Greek port of Piraeus, where much of eastern Mediterranean shipping is based, and look for a ship. It was very much a learning experience. There were times of fasting by missing an evening meal, spending the time just to be still before the Lord, really seeking His face to know what to do. I came close to agreement for a newly refurbished Greek ferry ship, in many ways very suitable for our purposes, although the cabins were somewhat smaller than I would have liked and had shared toilet facilities.

'I admit that I still feel that we have not yet got the right ship,' I said in a taped message to our supporters. 'I had hoped to get a real release regarding the ship in my spirit.' But I felt an urgency to press ahead, use the permissions we had been granted and gain practical experience before signing a long-term contract. At the last minute, however, the owners of the ship telexed a withdrawal of their offer to England, without any explanation. I was back to square one and somehow I had a peace about it. I felt the Lord had intervened and that there would be a better vessel. It was training to wait for His perfect timing.

I returned to Piraeus again and visited ship after ship. I still remember taking the launch out to the *Mediterranean Sky*. It was a huge ship and the only way on board was up a rope ladder hanging over the side. I clung tightly as the ladder swayed over the choppy water 30 feet below and finally put a leg up and climbed over the railing on to the deck. It surpassed all the others we had seen, a beautiful vessel with capacity for 900 passengers plus a crew of 120. It was a bigger, better, but also more expensive vessel than I had bargained for. Rex Worth, chief ship engineer with Operation Mobilisation, who was accompanying me on this trip, got very excited. 'This is the ship!' he exclaimed.

But I said, 'Lord, I must know from you.' I value counsel and am so grateful for it, but to make critical decisions I need to hear from the Lord myself. I was a bit shocked and surprised at a ship that big. I asked the Lord for a sign. That same day back at the shipping office, He reminded me that the Living Bible renders Isaiah 60:9:

> *'I have reserved the ships of many lands, the very best, to bring the sons of Israel home again from far away, bringing their wealth with them.'*

And I suddenly knew the Lord was saying, 'the best.' I had peace. We reached an oral agreement on chartering the vessel for three trial sailings.

I went to Jerusalem to try to close an agreement on this ship with the business consortium. The Israelis are great bureaucrats. I sat in meeting after meeting. Some went on for six to eight hours. The lawyers were experts in highlighting all that could possibly go wrong. All they managed was to turn one problem into half a dozen problems. Steve, as always, was ready with a quip: 'It will take a parting of the red tape for this exodus!'

Finally, at the end of November, we reached an agreement. I was exhausted. What a battle! The terms were not as good as I would have liked, but I believed it had the Lord's approval. We agreed to meet after the weekend to exchange contracts.

But when I turned up three of the four consortium members had cold feet. 'Gustav, we need to postpone,' one told me. 'We would like you to postpone by a few months.'

I had doubts in my spirit about waiting. I felt we had to go ahead. I told them I needed 48 hours. I wanted to enquire of the Lord. I made half a dozen phone calls all over the world to trusted intercessors who were identifying with us and said, 'This is the position: should we sail now or should we postpone?'

I waited all day for an answer. I was under such pressure. It was ten o'clock at night when Ted turned up again to encourage me. As I was sharing my dilemma the phone started to ring. Within an hour all six from all over the world rang, one after the other, and said, 'Gustav, now is the time. Hallelujah!'

Reluctantly the consortium members agreed and I returned to Piraeus to sign for the ship. But a phone call came from our lawyer in Jerusalem. 'Gustav, you cannot sign,' he said emphatically. 'Things are not ripened. The consortium cannot provide services. The entire deal is cancelled or postponed for an indefinite period.' I had to pack my suitcase and return to England. I was devastated.

As I got to my office in Bournemouth the phone rang and a man who was helping us to gather the Jews in Odessa said in desperation, 'Gustav, we have 500 registered to sail. Some of them have already arrived. They have given up their home, their jobs. You must sail!' What a situation to be in.

As I listened for the leading of the Lord there came a clear inner conviction: 'Yes, you go now.' I just knew the Lord wanted us to move ahead.

I returned to Jerusalem, where to my surprise most of the consortium members were still ready to work with us and we came to terms on a revised contract. It was then time to finalize our agreement with the owner of the *Mediterranean Sky*. I rang Steve in Seattle and said, 'Steve, this is so big. I need your help.' I was so grateful that he agreed to come with me to Piraeus to sign the contract.

And so we went back to the enormous plush office of the ship owner, beautifully filled with paintings and models of seagoing vessels. You knew you were in the office of a tycoon. Steve and I sat at the table with him and the manager of his company and over a meal discussed amendments to the contract. The negotiations became intense. 'I'm not going to do anything!' the manager shouted at one point, and stormed out of the room.

It seemed that everything that could go wrong had. There is just one thing that stands out in my mind. I was due to sign for three sailings, a commitment for several hundred thousand dollars that Ebenezer didn't have. I would be personally responsible with all that I had as collateral. I sat there looking at this contract and it seemed to me that the figures were getting bigger and bigger. My faith was wavering, and I was thinking, 'Lord, what should I do?' I was perplexed.

Steve started weeping next to me. Later he told me that after so many setbacks he was thinking, 'Lord, is this the end? Should we just get up and walk away from this table?' He didn't speak; he was just crying and crying.

And as I sat there a peace came over me. I knew what I had to do.

I said, 'I will sign.'

And as I signed, Steve jumped up and shouted, 'Hallelujah! Hallelujah!'

'What is happening now?' I asked.

And then he said, 'Gustav, can't you see all the angels? This room is full of angels and they are all applauding that we have signed this contract. It will be recorded in heavenly journals.'

I didn't see the angels. But I had such joy, such a release in my spirit. I put my hand on the contract and said, 'Now we are going to pray that the Lord will watch over, protect, and bless this shipping operation.'

The shipping tycoon, an imposing figure with aristocratic features, was watching all this. I am sure he had never experienced anything like it before. He took out his pen and made the sign of the cross on top of the contract. Operation Exodus was born!

CHAPTER 4

Lord of the Breakthrough

'So the redeemed of the LORD shall return,
And come to Zion with singing,
With everlasting joy on their heads.
They shall obtain joy and gladness,
And sorrow and sighing shall flee away.'

Isaiah 51:11

Only two weeks remained between the signing and the first of three sailings of the *Mediterranean Sky*. But before Elsa and I rushed off to coordinate preparations in Odessa, we met with some of the growing number of intercessors who were part of this operation. We knew we were in for a battle and wanted to make them aware of the significance of this undertaking: opening the first holy highway from the Soviet Union to Israel.

Years before the Lord had sent a remarkable man to teach Elsa and me that intercession was at the heart of our calling to help the Jewish people home. A letter came from a staff member of the Bible College of Wales inviting me to come and speak about the return of God's chosen people. I had no desire to go. I felt inadequate to speak at a school of the standing of the Bible College of Wales. It had been raised up from nothing 50 years before by Rees Howells, the Welsh coal miner who gave himself to the Holy Spirit and went on to shake the Church with his intercession.

I groped for an excuse. 'Please write and tell them that the date is not convenient,' I told Beverley.

A second letter came offering an alternative date. I couldn't make up my mind. But when I went to an Israel Day sponsored by Prayer for Israel and greeted the ministry's founder, Ken Burnett, he said just one thing: 'When are you going to visit the Bible College of Wales?'

The visit turned out to be one of the great blessings of my life. The college's little meeting hall was packed that evening and when I finished speaking Samuel Howells, son of Rees Howells, came up. 'We have prayed for the return of the Jews to the Promised Land for many, many years,' he said.

Our guest room that night was opposite the room of Dr Kingsley Priddy, headmaster of the grammar school attached to the Bible College. He was a medical doctor who had prepared to serve the Lord in Africa, but was surprised instead by His call to assist Rees Howells at the college. He was quite an imposing man, an English gentleman, but with a kind face and clear blue eyes that seemed almost to look through you.

As we were talking he mentioned that he had a niece on the south coast of England near our home. 'If you'd ever like to combine a trip to see her with an overnight in Bournemouth, you'd be a most welcome guest,' I told him.

Many visits followed. Kingsley adopted us as his family and we spent precious evenings together. He had countless stories to tell from his life and from the days with Rees Howells, who gave up his money, his food, his reputation and even risked his life to successfully intercede for others. Kingsley stood with Rees during the war years, as the little band at the college believed the Holy Spirit was influencing world events through their prayers.

Kingsley helped us see that our role in the ingathering was like that of Daniel 2,500 years before (see Daniel 9). Daniel understood from reading the book of Jeremiah that the time had come for the Jewish people to return from their limited exile in Babylon. He stood in their place, identified with them and allowed the Holy Spirit to intercede through him to accomplish what God had purposed to do.

Sunday December 15th 1991 is a day printed deep in my heart. We took leave from our fellowship, packed and talked to our children over the phone. Elsa and I were leaving at four o'clock the following morning for Ukraine. At 10:30 that night the phone rang. It was one of the Israeli lawyers.

'Gustav, the permit you have for your shipping line qualifies you to carry tourists and freight, but it does not qualify you to carry immigrants. We need an endorsement. You **must** delay.' He was terrified that we would arrive in Odessa and not be able to take one Jew with us. Our operation would become a laughing stock.

I stood there a minute, phone in hand, and pondered the situation. Our volunteers had started gathering in Piraeus. The shipping company had assembled the crew. The Jews had started to arrive in Odessa. And I had a sense the Lord had given the green light.

'No, we will sail,' I told him.

The lawyer's voice came back over the line. 'It's on your shoulders, Gustav.'

I alerted the intercessors. But that night I didn't sleep much.

In the morning we flew to Kiev and a lovely Christian girl picked us up at the airport to take us to the station for a train to Odessa. She was working with the Exobus project, bussing *olim* to meet Jewish Agency flights. We had hardly left the airport when a policeman stopped us. He came to the window of the car and began speaking rapidly in Russian.

'What does he want? What is he saying?' I asked our escort.

'He wants some money or something,' she said. 'He says we've been speeding.'

'In this old car and the road in this condition? It's impossible to speed!' I exclaimed.

She handed the officer a pair of nylon stockings through the window. To my amazement he pocketed them and walked off. She explained this was a common way for the police to increase their meagre income. 'We often take something with us when we go out so we can move on quickly when we're stopped.'

It was the first sign of the chaotic conditions we found facing us. Elsa and I checked into the Londonskaya hotel in Odessa, an aristocratic building with imposing corridors and stained glass windows. It was considered the city's best hotel, but for several days we had no heating and for two days we had no water. The windows were uninsulated and our huge room was an icebox.

As there was no dining room we joined the city residents in the daily search for food, and felt with our own stomachs the still-devastating effect of the famine and economic collapse that had struck the land. Walking down the frozen streets we passed food shop windows decorated with curtains and lights – but they were empty. One of the largest markets had nothing but dusty bottles of a pickled vegetable and a few wrinkled apples that were rotting away. At home they would have gone in the rubbish bin.

Great crowds converged on shops where it was possible to buy one of two staples: bread and vodka, the narcotic with which many drowned their problems. Elsa would queue up for half an hour to buy a loaf of bread, which we would eat with cheese or a sausage in our room. But food did not seem important to us. We felt privileged to be there. These were historic days.

The ship was on its way to Odessa, but with three days to go we were still without the right papers. I learned what pressure means. It was a nightmare to see hundreds of Jewish people gathering with their families and baggage – having left behind their jobs and homes – and not knowing if we would be able to take them.

We were trying to do something during the last dying days

of the Soviet Union. The giant had been brought to its knees. The republics had declared their independence and Gorbachev, unwilling to use force against them, was now a powerless figurehead. Already in many cities the statues of Lenin encircled by the intercessors years before were coming down. As we sought permission for our operation we would talk one day with one group, only to find the next day they were not even in power. The only way we knew to deal with it was on our knees, down on the wooden floor of the frigid hotel room. Elsa and I cried out to the Lord.

Then two men showed up at the port in suits and ties – consuls sent from the Israeli embassy in Moscow. They helped in sensitive negotiations. We received the permission to board *olim* from the port authorities 36 hours before the sailing. It was such a victory – *36 hours before the sailing!* Until that time we didn't know whether or not the Jewish people would be able to board the ship.

They were spread over the whole terminal building with their mountains of luggage, sleeping on their bags for up to three nights while waiting to go through customs. It was cold and draughty, but they did not grumble. Their resilience greatly impressed me.

Many had struggled to make it to Odessa from all over the Soviet Union: 55 airports were closed because of a shortage of petrol. We booked a charter flight to bring a group of 98 out of Baku. We had the plane but we just couldn't get the fuel. They decided instead to come by train for the third sailing. We had another group booked from Moldova, but were prevented from sending buses for them by armed conflict in the region.

Everybody had tried to cash in on the *olim* as they made the journey to Odessa – whether the train conductor, the porter, the taxi driver. They all had stories of exorbitant prices and broken promises along the trek from their homes to the port. 'Someone wanted to warm his hands on our grief,' said Nahum, a sculptor, quoting a Russian proverb.

So when they realized who we were and why we were there, they warmly embraced us. There is a special bond in time of crisis. We were their link to the outside world. We had brought hope to their lives.

We tried to bring them refreshments. But each time we gave them mineral water they would open their luggage and offer us in return one of their precious bottles of vodka. '*Spaseeba, spaseeba,*' they thanked us, and motioned for us to sit with them on their luggage and share some of their smoked fish and bread.

'Why are you going to Israel?' Elsa asked them as they waited. Many said they were fleeing the effects of Chernobyl. Elsa confessed to me that at first she was disappointed this was their reason. 'I expected them to go because they are Jews,' she told me. 'I said, "Lord, I can't believe that they don't understand why they are going at all!"'

Then she saw a bride in a long traditional white gown walking through the port building with her groom on their way to a wedding reception and was reminded of Revelation 19:7–9. She felt the Lord said, 'That's right, they don't understand, but they're going back for a wedding, the marriage of the Lamb of God.'

There were mountains of luggage at the port, thousands of pieces. The Jewish people in the land of the north had few suitcases, so they brought their things in cartons, bags, even in curtains tied up with string. It was so moving to see. There were television sets, carpets – it seemed to me that each one took full advantage of the 500-kilogramme luggage allowance. Some of it was rubbish, but they were so attached to it. That was one of the reasons we wanted to bring them home by ship, so they could truly take their belongings with them. It would make their start in Israel so much easier.

But as yet one obstacle loomed between the *olim* and their new life: the customs hall. They were all frightened to go through customs – and Elsa and I soon saw why.

Communism was dying in name only. The hardness of pharaoh's heart was still reflected in the cruel system and hard faces of many of the customs personnel. Every single item was opened as the officials methodically and without compromise carried out their instructions. Every page of every book was checked for hidden banknotes. All this took hours for each family.

Those leaving were regarded as traitors to their country – and treated as such. They were not allowed to take out anything of real value. I saw a woman whose little son had asthma; his medicine was taken away. An 18-year-old girl came to me with her mother. 'Could you take for me a little sewing machine?' she sobbed. I couldn't – it would risk the authorities closing us down completely.

Customs officers took jewellery away, sometimes forcibly – the flesh of one woman's finger was torn when a tight-fitting gold ring was forced from her hand. 'Jews go out with all the best things,' the officer told her. 'This is why the Soviet Union is poor.' Another woman sobbed hysterically all the way to the ship after her grandmother's heirloom wedding ring was taken from her. Wheelchairs, medicines, nappies, baby food and even family photographs were confiscated – the latter on the grounds of 'national security'.

A middle-aged artist was even refused permission to take out her own paintings on the grounds that 'a work of art is a national treasure.' She wept as her life's work was taken away. Like many she was uncertain at that moment that she was doing the right thing. I put a hand gently on her shoulder. 'Life is more than material things,' I said through an interpreter. 'You have followed the God of Israel and He will bless you for it.'

What they didn't leave behind was their education. When I first met the mayor of Odessa, himself Jewish, he made a truthful accusation against us: 'You're taking some of my finest people.' Many of the Soviet Jews were highly trained engineers, doctors, or musicians.

The story went around Ben Gurion airport that a man asked the porter, 'I see almost everyone has a violin case or a guitar or something, but there are a few who have no musical instruments. What are they doing?' The porter turned round and said, 'That is very simply explained – they are the pianists.'

Sailing day finally arrived. Elsa and I rose before dawn and made our way down the great stone staircase leading to the port in the biting winter wind and heavy fog. There was the *Mediterranean Sky*!

It was an awesome sight. The ship was brightly lit, four decks glowing in vibrant gold, orange and white, stretching over 160 metres. It was by far the largest vessel we had seen in Odessa since our arrival. It seemed like a visitor from another world in the drab port. After all the tensions and immense pressure of the days gone by I couldn't help but some tears ran down my face – tears of joy and tears of relief.

Steve was on board with 20 volunteers. As the ship came in they sounded a ram's horn known as a *shofar*, blown by Jewish people since the time of Moses as a call of liberation. *Olim* leapt up from the piles of luggage they'd been guarding through the night and ran out of the building shouting and waving.

'How great You are, O God,' my heart sang as I thought of Psalm 147, 'How majestic You are, because what You have proposed, that which is written, You fulfil. You gather together the outcasts of Israel. You heal the broken-hearted and bind up their wounds.'

We really saw a great gathering boarding the ship – 550 in all – the old and the young, the woman with child, the lame and the blind. It was just how Jeremiah 31 described it. They came up the ramp to the ship with their dogs, cats, with their birds in cages. We witnessed many moving goodbyes and saw tears as the Soviet Jews took leave of the only land they'd ever known.

The *Mediterranean Sky* pulled away after midnight. What a wonderful sight to see it float out of the harbour with all the lights. It was finally done. Christians had opened the sea route for Jewish people from the Soviet Union to Israel!

Two days later Elsa and I celebrated Christmas on our own in Odessa. At 7:00 o'clock that evening Gorbachev appeared on television. 'I hereby discontinue my activities at the post of President of the Union of Soviet Socialist Republics,' he announced, and with him disappeared the Soviet Union. That night the red flag was lowered from the Kremlin. It was six years to the week since the proclamation of the intercessors outside his office.

The *Mediterranean Sky* was crossing 1150 nautical miles in close to gale force weather. Finally on the fourth morning the storm lifted and the port city of Haifa came in sight, bathed in golden sun. The captain sounded the booming foghorn and police boats rushed out to greet the ship with lights and sirens. *Olim* leaned over the railing, looking at their Promised Land. No one knew whether to laugh or cry.

Concerns about a possible terrorist attack on the vessel led to the Israeli military censor suppressing news reports of the voyage. That same week at the Jewish Agency transit camp in Budapest a car bomb just missed a bus full of *olim* and killed an escorting policeman. But in the morning Israel Radio broadcast the news of the ship's arrival and a crowd of journalists and well-wishers stood waiting ashore.

There was applause, cheering, the playing of a band and the sound of rubber squeaking against rubber as the ship made contact with the dock. Cameras flashed as those on shore leaned back to photograph the ship towering above them. Minister of Absorption Yitzhak Peretz, himself an Orthodox rabbi, could not hide his excitement as he came on board to greet the *olim*. 'You have arrived home, to your family, to your home,' he told them. 'The government of Israel will do all that is possible to help you in your new home.'

He kissed a nine-year-old boy called Genia, whose father introduced the rest of the family and said, 'We are happy that we have arrived to Israel. We waited very long for this moment.'

'When I saw the coast of Israel from the ship I was so excited that I couldn't speak,' added Sophia, an English teacher from the republic of Georgia. 'I believe that it will be good here. It has to be good.'

One of the first *olim* to step off the ship was still clutching his maroon Soviet passport, together with the dark blue Israeli immigration book he'd received from officials on board the ship. '*Shalom, shalom!*' he cried excitedly.

'I can't tell you what this means,' said an Israeli on the dock who'd helped to gather the *olim* in Odessa. 'I lost my whole family in Europe. If there had been more ships like this, it would have been a different story.'

'Ship brings Jews in new exodus' read the headline on the Associated Press story, which appeared in newspapers around the world. The arrival was on the front page of all the major Israeli newspapers and brought back bittersweet memories for many. In the 1930s and 40s nearly every Jewish newcomer arrived via the Mediterranean. The best-known ship, the *Exodus*, was intercepted in 1947 by British forces attempting to enforce strict immigration quotas. Three Jewish passengers were killed by British fire and some 100 wounded.

Now we had opportunity to publicly stand with the homecoming of the Jewish people. 'These are Christians that love Israel,' our lawyer explained to an interviewer for the national television news. 'They see the significance of the return of the people to the land.'

Johannes and Kjell were also there at Haifa to welcome Steve. 'Both Kjell and I wept when we saw the ship coming in,' Johannes said later. 'It was the most moving experience of all my time as an intercessor. Looking back at what we did on the stairs in Odessa six years earlier, and seeing all these Jews and the enormous mountain of luggage – to realize that God really did honour what we did, that little group. I didn't even have faith for it when we were there. I felt it was insane what we did. But we were on to a prophetic act of God.

'Incredible! Everything we did came to pass. Everything.'

CHAPTER 5

'None of Them Will Be Left Behind'

'I have chosen you and have not cast you away.'
Isaiah 41:9

I was just astounded when the telex from our attorney came in after the docking in Haifa:

'Dear Gustav,
We have just had a most serious complaint from the Ministry of Absorption, which not only threatens to abort our whole operation, but can lead to extremely unpleasant and far-reaching consequences.
Some of the Israeli officials on board complained that they witnessed what certainly amounts to missionary activity. On many occasions several of the immigrants were invited to visit and contact the Christians in Jerusalem.'

I had never given any serious thought to the matter. Our guidelines to the team had been clear. We didn't try to preach to the *olim*. We just loved them. The Lord had shown me that we were simply to show them love in action and do our best to help bring them back. I had put this in writing for the Israeli government. If we broke our commitment they would bring the line to a halt and we would have failed in what God had called us to carry out.

The *Mediterranean Sky* was returning to Odessa for the second sailing and the Absorption Ministry demanded that all volunteers be confined to their cabins until they could be removed in Haifa. I went on board the ship when it arrived back in Odessa and gathered the volunteers in a lounge.

'All who are willing to honour our commitment,' I told them, 'I want you to stand to your feet now. We will not be missionaries by words, but we want to be ambassadors by our actions. Each one of you make this declaration before the Lord. If not, get off the ship now.'

All stood to their feet. That gave me confidence that I had a team I could trust and enabled me to take a clear stand on the issue in the face of government pressure.

Certainly the charge showed some misunderstanding of our motives. But it's equally important that we understand the mind of the Jewish people on this point. For millennia they have resisted efforts aimed at their elimination. Not a few heroically chose death rather than deny the faith of their fathers. The apocryphal books of the Maccabees record the stirring story of the fight against assimilation in the second century BC which preserved Israel and made possible the subsequent birth of the Messiah.

My own children – of Swiss parents but born in Great Britain – are more British than Swiss. But the Jews have survived as a distinct people while scattered among the nations for nearly 2,000 years. It is nothing less than the hand of God, who promised in Jeremiah 31:36 that the sun and the moon would depart before '*the seed of Israel shall also cease from being a nation before Me forever.*' Jewish people feel deeply – and rightly – that it is evil to attempt to turn a Jew into a non-Jew.

And in the minds of a majority of the Jewish people **to believe in Jesus is to become a non-Jew.**

> 'The stone that the builders rejected
> Has become the chief cornerstone.'
>
> Psalm 118:22

> 'Hardening in part has happened to Israel until the fullness of
> the Gentiles has come in.'
>
> Romans 11:25

This explains the emotional vulnerability of the Israelis to rumours that we were 'missionising'. In their minds arose the horrifying image of these precious *olim* buttonholed in their cabins by zealous Christians urging them to convert and stop being Jews!

Only in recent decades have growing numbers of Jews – like Steve Lightle – recaptured the historical and biblical truth that Jesus and His first followers were practicing Jews who upheld the *Torah*, and that faith in Jesus as Messiah can be expressed without leaving the Jewish people. How ironic to the reader of the New Testament book of Acts, who knows that the debate raging among the earliest followers of Jesus was whether Gentiles could believe without first becoming Jews!

In fact we came under attack on this issue from believers as well. It's been painful. A lovely young couple, both Jewish believers in Messiah, came to our hotel room in Odessa. They wanted to come to the port to speak to the *olim* and couldn't accept our position. But Elsa and I take comfort from the Word of God. Ezekiel 36 clearly states that after the Lord brings back His people He will then sprinkle them with water and give them a new heart and new spirit. And just as the first exodus led to the giving of the law, Jeremiah 31 links the final exodus with the making of a new covenant with the house of Israel.

Meanwhile something **was** being communicated to the *olim* and Israeli officials as the volunteers remained on board for the second sailing. It began as our team in Odessa made trip after trip up the ramp to the ship, helping the immigrants with their heavy baggage. They served drinks to the *olim* as they boarded, taught them elementary Hebrew and Israeli songs – even tore up sheets for the infants after the Odessa customs officials went so far as to confiscate all disposable nappies!

Then the night before docking in Haifa the volunteers held a shipboard celebration for the *olim*. Carol Cantrell, a worship leader from Jerusalem, led them in Hebrew songs, many of them from the *Tanakh* (Old Testament). Two Israeli women who were on board left their government group and came and sat at Carol's feet to sing and clap, their faces beaming. In the middle of the lounge a dancing circle formed of Christians, Israelis and *olim* – one of them the woman who had wept over her ring while boarding the ship, now transformed.

'I felt there was a moment when the burden lifted off them and was replaced with joy,' Carol said later. 'It says so clearly in Scripture they'll come back with rejoicing and singing.'

Everyone stood for the singing of the Israeli national anthem *HaTikvah* (The Hope), and Carol finished with *Shalom, chaverim* (Farewell, friends) as the *olim* went out with tear-streaked faces, some trying to communicate the warmth of their feeling by sending kisses across the room to the volunteers.

'In Russia we knew Jewish people have only enemies in the world,' said one. 'We didn't know of any friends.'

'We have never experienced anything like this in our life,' another said in a tearful goodbye.

What a picture of Jewish-Christian reconciliation!

Later that night the six dark-haired Israeli security men filed into the small lounge on the bow of the ship where volunteers were meeting. With a prod from his partners, one spoke up: 'We just want to say *kol hakavod* (literally "all the honour") to you.'

As they left, Steve led the volunteers in prayer: '*Kol hakavod* to you, Lord.'

I started to relax as the third sailing date approached. Once again we had over 500 *olim* gathered. As with the previous sailings, the customs hall opened three days before departure. Our shipping agent came to me after the first day. 'Only 70 cleared today,' he said. 'It looks like the customs officials want to teach you a lesson.' He felt they were delaying the procedures so that not all the *olim* would be able to embark on the last sailing.

Elsa and I had planned to join this sailing to Israel. But I felt we were responsible for every Jew who had come to Odessa. 'If all the *olim* are not able to board you will have to go ahead on your own,' I told her. 'I'll stay behind to arrange a flight or come up with some other solution.'

We started to cry to the Lord so that He would make a way. 'Lord, these are your people, this is your operation,' I prayed. 'We need a miracle.' I knew if it went on like this customs clearance would take another six or seven days. And in fact the next day they again cleared only 70 – and the same on the third day.

So on the day of departure we still had about 300 people to go through customs in one day. That night I didn't sleep well and at about 3:00 a.m. I had radio contact with Steve on board the ship and shared the situation with him. He woke up the whole team and told them that instead of sleeping they should come on their knees and intercede for all the *olim* to board the sailing.

The phone rang at 3:30 a.m. and it was a sister from England.

'Gustav, I've been trying for hours to get through to you,' she said excitedly. 'The Lord has given me a word for you. I knew I had to pass it on this very night.' She was adamant. 'Would you turn to Zechariah, chapter 4, verses 6 to 7.'

I opened my Bible and read:

> *"'Not by might, nor by power, but by My Spirit,"*
> *says the LORD of hosts.*
> *"Who are you, O great mountain?*
> *Before Zerubbabel you shall become a plain!"'*

She didn't know what the mountain was. But I knew the moment I heard it that God had spoken. He would level the mountain of customs that exalted itself against Him.

I said to Elsa, 'Please pack my suitcase as well. We will both be on the ship.'

We managed to sleep an hour, then checked out of the hotel early in the morning with all our belongings and went down to the port. The *Mediterranean Sky* was in and Elsa and I boarded.

There was a different atmosphere on this sailing. The Absorption Ministry had sent a team of ultra-orthodox Jews from a *yeshiva* (seminary) to investigate the rumours of 'missionising'. Their leader was Chaim, a self-assured 25-year-old former immigrant who had been arrested by the KGB at 15 for Zionist activity. 'You can have **nothing** to do with the *olim*,' he told us at the outset. Reporters from Israeli newspapers were also present to report on the tension.

Among the first passengers to come on board was an elderly couple. They had been three or four days in the terminal and were extremely traumatized. It was the Sabbath and the religious Jews could do nothing to help process them. Our volunteers had to come forward. Two of our team were standing at the top of the gangplank with hot chocolate. Just behind them one of the Orthodox men was watching what they would do.

The man put his arm around the shoulder of the elderly man and the lady volunteer put her arm around the woman's shoulder. This expression of love affected the two so much they broke down and sobbed. The volunteers just put their arms around them. Suddenly the expression of the Orthodox man, who had been quite hostile, changed and softened.

Throughout the day a slow trickle of *olim* cleared customs and boarded the ship. We were scheduled to leave that evening, but late in the afternoon more than 250 were still waiting in the hall. 'A day's delay in port would cost us between 20,000 and 25,000 dollars,' I told our team. 'We have to sail on time.'

I asked the intercessors on board to pray while Steve and I went to the ship salon to meet with the Israeli consuls and the captain. Anxiety was written on the faces of all in the room as I laid out for them the situation. Then Eliyahu Ben Haim, the leader of the intercessors, came to the door and called me outside. 'We've had a clear word from Ezekiel 39:28,' he said. 'None of them will be left behind.'

I received it immediately. Money considerations went out – I knew it was the Lord. I returned to the officials.

'This is what the Lord said,' I told them, opening the Bible. 'He will leave none of them behind. We will wait until all are on board.'

As we wrestled against opposition we were learning to proclaim the promises of God from the Scriptures for the Jewish people and the *aliyah*. *'Is not my word like a fire?'* says the Lord in Jeremiah 23:29, *'and like a hammer that breaks the rock in pieces?'*

We realized many in the terminal would not board the ship that night, and had spent hours or even days waiting with little food. The ship's staff graciously prepared a fish dinner and our volunteers set up tables right in the building. All were able to eat well that night. The captain said later he was proud to be part of what was written in the Bible!

We had to delay the sailing for 27 hours. In the end they needed the port for another vessel and made us leave. But everyone was on board – with every piece of luggage. And I praised the Lord for it. We stood our ground and God gained a tremendous victory, establishing in the heavenlies that nothing could hold back even one of the *olim*.

Elsa and I were utterly exhausted. On board ship was the first night in many nights that we really had a good sleep. It felt like paradise after the battle we'd been through every day, every hour in Odessa. The ship seemed to be a dream: warm bath, fresh food and nice tablecloths ... all the things we once took for granted. I thought of Psalm 126:

> 'When the LORD brought back the captives to Zion,
>   we were like men who dreamed.
> Our mouths were filled with laughter,
>   our tongues with songs of joy.'
>
> Psalm 126:1–2 (NIV)

We indeed had a sense of deep joy and satisfaction as we stood on deck the next morning and looked at the Black Sea stretching off to the overcast horizon.

But we were soon to be reminded that this had indeed been a black sea for the Jews. Some weeks before I'd heard for the first time the horrifying story of another immigrant ship, the *Struma*, which had passed through these same waters exactly 50 years before us. I went to the archives in Jerusalem to get information and pictures, which I shared with our volunteers. And once we knew what had happened we all felt we had to do something about it on this sailing.

Fleeing the Holocaust in Romania, 769 Jews had set sail in the *Struma*, a tiny, 100-year-old cattle barge meant only for river navigation. After four days of intermittent engine breakdowns they somehow made it to Istanbul harbour, where they sought permission from the British mandatory authorities to enter Palestine (pre-state Israel).

Instead they became part of one of the saddest chapters of British history. While millions were perishing in the Holocaust during the 1939 – 1945 War, those Jews who tried to escape were denied entry to the 'national home' the British government had promised them just two decades before. The British informed the Turkish authorities that the Jews from the *Struma* would not be admitted to Palestine and asked that they not be allowed into Turkey either.

The ship languished in the freezing harbour for weeks under unimaginable conditions. The Jews were packed below deck without room even to lie down. There was only one makeshift toilet and no bathing facilities for 769 people. Women were giving birth on board.

On the ship's 35th day in Istanbul the Nazis convened the Wannsee conference in suburban Berlin to decide upon 'the final solution to the Jewish problem,' no doubt taking into account the indifference of the democracies. The Jewish Agency made numerous appeals on behalf of the *Struma* passengers, but Britain still refused to yield. On the 70th day the Turks towed the ship back into the Black Sea and left the Jews without food, water or fuel. The next morning an explosion was heard and the ship disappeared beneath the water. Only one passenger survived.

A group of our volunteers from Britain resolved to hold an on-board ceremony of memorial and repentance as we passed through the Black Sea. Their desire was to stand before God and seek His forgiveness for their nation's part in the tragedy – and ask the Jews for their forgiveness. But the Orthodox Jews on board did not want any *olim* to participate. They were very agitated, debating loudly in their cabins until 3 a.m. the night before. We chose not to argue. We were there to serve them.

We came together for the ceremony on the rear of the ship with only the Israeli reporters, photographers, and government officials witnessing the scene. Drops of rain wet the faces of a dozen British Christians as they stood in a semi-circle in the freezing Black Sea wind. Fred Wright, then a minister in Colchester, spoke in a choked voice: 'We from England are standing here to request forgiveness for the hardheartedness and lack of compassion that our country showed to the passengers of the *Struma*. This was a sinful act and we humbly ask for forgiveness.'

We stood together in silence for two minutes as the waters churned behind us. The British believers had prepared a huge wreath – as tall as they were – from flowers and pine branches broken down the previous week by a rare snowstorm in Jerusalem. Two of them carried it to the railing and tossed it into the sea. There was a long, solemn sounding of the ship's horn, as the crew, in dress uniform, saluted the ship's flag, which flew at half-mast.

It was so moving. Many were crying. The Israelis became part of the ceremony. Several with tear-streaked faces found themselves quite spontaneously embracing the British Christians. 'If you believe and love us this way, it gives us hope for the future,' one said.

Veteran journalist Aviezer Golan, a writer for Israel's leading daily, served as a volunteer in the British army at the time of the sinking of the *Struma*. 'I was the least emotional of the lot,' he said afterwards, 'and I felt very moved. Definitely there was a feeling of coming closer.' He opened his published report on the sailing with a vivid description of the scene.

'It was about eternal and spiritual issues,' explained Bob Hobbs, pastor of an English house church. 'We wanted to settle this and show our hearts. We believe that something happened there that was important to God, and important to the relationship between Israel and England in some way.'

'There was a time for both of us when Israel was just a nation,' added his wife Delphine, 'when my attitude to them was just like any other nation. Even as a born-again believer I didn't have understanding of His glorious purposes for Israel. Progressively He gave me understanding. He began to open

Wearing gas masks at the International Prayer Conference
in Jerusalem in 1991, during the first Gulf War.

Gustav & Elsa Scheller, founders of Ebenezer Operation Exodus.

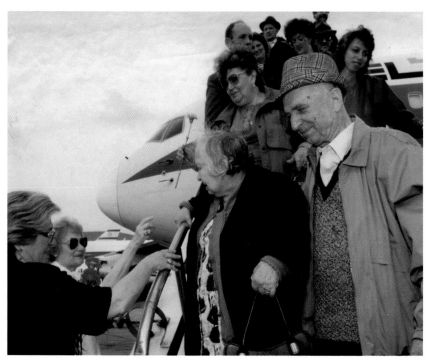

Olim arriving in Israel on one of the first Ebenezer flights.

A welcome ceremony for new olim in Israel.

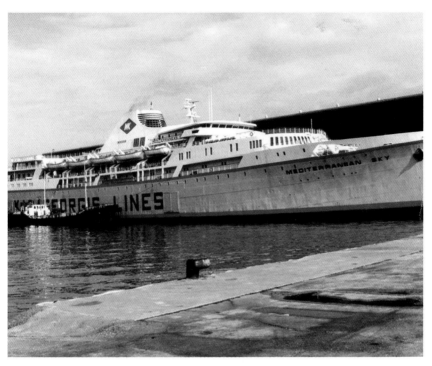

The Mediterranean Sky –
chartered in 1991 for 3 trial sailings between Odessa and Haifa.

Ebenezer staff and volunteers on one of the aliyah sailings between Odessa and Haifa.

Ebenezer workers visiting Jewish families in their home
in the former Soviet Union and sharing about aliyah.

A happy family on their way to a new life in Israel.

Ebenezer team helping olim at the railway station on their way to Israel.

Demonstrating 'love in action' by bringing humanitarian aid.

Often our teams have to travel long distances to remote regions in harsh conditions to find Jewish families.

A Jewish man and his daughter making aliyah from South Africa.

A group of new olim at the Western Wall showing their new Israeli identity cards.

A Jewish family who made aliyah from the USA at the Western Wall.

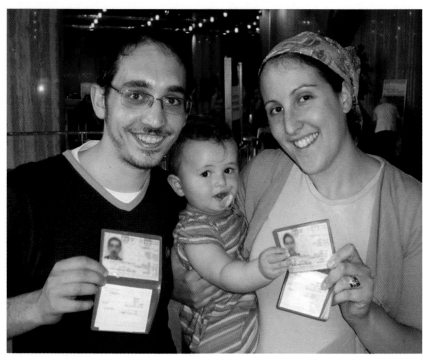

A happy Jewish family from the UK with their Israeli identity cards.

Young adults service project on Engage Israel.

His heart to me and touch mine. Now Israel is a very special place for me, and I have a real love for the Jews in my heart. My understanding of the Scriptures – Tanakh and New Testament – has dramatically changed. So now I am very much allied with Israel, with the homecoming of the Jews and God's purpose with them until Messiah returns.'

England is not the only nation that turned its back on the Jewish people. In 1938 the Evian conference was held. Thirty-two nations gathered to discuss the plight of the Jews. Before the conference Hitler threw out a challenge to them:

'I can only hope and expect that the other world, which has such deep sympathy for these criminals, will at least be generous enough to convert this sympathy into practical aid. We, on our part, are ready to put all these criminals at the disposal of these countries, for all I care, even on luxury ships.'

One nation after another washed its hands and made the Holocaust possible. The United States set the tone by pledging only to honour its existing miniscule quotas. Less than a year later in a widely publicized incident the American government refused to accept a boatload of 1,100 German Jewish refugees. They were forced back to Europe, where few survived the war. My own people, the Swiss, who took in many thousands of Jewish refugees in the war, closed their borders to an equal number who tried to escape from the Third Reich. They were pushed back over borders for a one-way journey to a concentration camp.

I believe there will not be one reading this whose home country has not done harm to the Jewish people in some way. Many of us have repented; but in my understanding this is only the first step. The Lord has clearly shown us in His word that we should carry the Jews back home to Israel. What an opportunity we have to say to the nation of Israel how deeply we care and so turn past curses into blessings!

CHAPTER 6

Death and Resurrection

'Deliver those who are drawn toward death,
And hold back those stumbling to the slaughter.'
Proverbs 24:11

'Now I know,' I began to think to myself after the first three sailings. 'I have served my apprenticeship.' It gave me security. Shipping had been new to me, but now I felt more confident. Later in the year I had a prompting in my spirit that it was time to renew the sailings on a regular basis. I had a sense that we should go with a vessel from a Russian company. The Black Sea Shipping Company (BLASCO) was at the time the biggest, I believe, in the world. They had 250 vessels. But when I told a shipping man that I wanted to charter with BLASCO, he dismissed it with a wave of his hand. 'BLASCO sends no ships to Israeli waters,' he said. 'Even tourists must change ships in Cyprus.' The president of the Black Sea Shipping Company, I learned, had no love for God's chosen people. He supported the former Soviet policy of boycotting the Jewish state.

So I went before the God of Israel and poured my heart out. I told him, 'This is not right.' And the Lord brought to my mind a word which King David pronounced many years ago over one of his enemies: *'Let his days be few, and let another take his office'* (Psalm 109:8). This was indeed a good word.

I went to the office of my shipping agent in Odessa. 'I want to send a telex to my office in England,' I told him, and sat at his desk and wrote: 'Let Christians around the world join me in prayer that Psalm 109:8 will apply to the president of BLASCO and he will be removed.'

I pushed this across the desk to the shipping agent, a young smartly dressed Ukrainian professional. He looked at it and was astounded. 'Are you sure?' he asked. 'It is not wise what you are doing.'

I understood him. There is never a sense of complete freedom in the former Soviet Union; people watch their speech far more carefully than we in the West. Sometimes associates would ask me to walk with them outside to discuss confidential matters. And the president of BLASCO was a powerful man in Ukraine.

'I am sure,' I said, nonetheless. I felt the Lord had given the release to do it.

Three days later Elsa and I were packing our suitcase at the hotel when I heard a knock on our door. I opened it to find the shipping agent. He looked at me and said, 'What kind of a man are you?'

'Why? What has happened?'

'This morning the news came on the radio – the president of the Black Sea Shipping Company is under investigation for corruption.'

The president was removed. His replacement was willing to work with us. We serve a great God!

Next came the challenge of finding a partner to handle the operation in Israel. I had quite hard discussions about this in January 1993 with shipping company owner Moshe Mano. We were miles apart following one long night in a lawyer's office in Tel Aviv.

Moshe offered to drive me to the central bus station so I could catch the midnight bus back to Jerusalem. He lost his way and at some traffic lights rolled down his window to ask directions from the next car. But instead he got excited, parked the car and jumped out. He talked very intently with the other driver for several minutes as I sat looking at my watch. I got a bit irritated, thinking I would miss the last bus. Finally he came back to the car.

'I've been trying to reach that man for several days,' he told me. 'His only son Ronen was shot in Hebron a month ago while on guard duty. There's a bullet still lodged in his brain.'

Moshe paused and looked over at me. 'You know, money is not that important,' he said. 'Life is important.'

We both knew that night there'd be no problem reaching an agreement. And in fact together we chartered the 500-bed BLASCO passenger ship *Dmitry Shostakovich* for 25 weekly sailings between April and September 1993. It was a beautiful ship, built in 1980 at the Gdansk shipyard where Lech Walesa, President of Poland 1990-95, worked as an electrician.

After long negotiations we also leased a former Communist youth camp in Odessa to house and feed the *olim* for several days before each sailing. Elsa and I moved in to coordinate the operation in mid-March while the grounds were still covered with snow. Volunteers began streaming in from many nations to serve with us.

At first we found the camp was a dark place. Strange characters went in and out of the hotel. We heard dogs barking all night and saw them limping about in the day as if they'd been beaten. The weather was freezing and the heating and hot water were often out of order. Most of the toilet seats were missing from the bathrooms. The food was awful. And unless a translator was with us the language barrier left us helpless.

The staff looked at us with cold suspicion. 'There's not much willingness to please,' Elsa commented to me after a few days. 'It's more like negotiating our rights.' I had to agree. The staff carried out their duties with empty, hard expressions, projecting their own difficult past. I did meet some Ukrainians during this time who went out of their way to be helpful. But that was certainly the rare exception and not the rule. When I looked into the eyes of the former Soviet people I could hardly

ever detect a sparkle and I couldn't help thinking how much
they needed Jesus.

We found everything was an effort in the post-Communist
Ukraine. Technologically they were 50 years behind the West.
It was easier to drive across town to someone than to reach
them by phone. One morning I needed to make photocopies.
There were two shops in town. I went to the first and found it
had no electricity. I crossed town to the second and found it
had no paper.

I took a translator with me and went down to the port. I
knew we'd have to come to some terms with the Ukrainian
customs officials if we were to avoid the scenes of the earlier
sailings. We faced 12 customs and immigration officials across
a long table in a frigid room.

I was a bit naive. 'We believe that we will carry as many as
8,000 emigrants on these sailings,' I told them. 'I've come to
see what your requirements are.'

There were no smiles. The temperature visibly dropped.

'We are not equipped for emigration,' the head official
replied grimly. 'If you want us to be, you must provide.' They
pulled out lists of demands that I estimated would cost
hundreds of thousands of dollars: x-ray equipment, computers
and building a storage room.

I declined our lawyer's offer to write to the Ukrainian
president about the customs impasse. Instead I turned to the
Lord. And after many battles and negotiations to the early
hours, we came to terms. Together with our Israeli shipping
agent we did indeed agree to purchase x-ray equipment, which
would allow customs to process the *olim* without the
painstaking opening of every bag. The new procedures would
cut a family's waiting time with their possessions from days to
three or four hours.

But even as one problem was sorted out, another came. No
ship insurance was in place. No approval had come from the
Ukrainian Foreign Ministry. No wood could be found to crate

the baggage. The equipment we had promised the customs officials didn't arrive. Word came from the Absorption Ministry in Israel that the first sailing date was unacceptable, as the ship would arrive just before the start of Passover, when the *Torah* allows no work. 'If it's late we'll leave it at sea with no provisions,' they warned. To top it all there was no fuel in the port for the sailing!

And then we found that the optimistic reports of the Ukrainian Jewish group responsible for recruiting *olim* were illusory. Only 43 were booked for the first sailing. It seemed all hell had been turned loose against this shipping line. Faith levels began to drop and a few volunteers began to lose heart and question our mission.

I felt that a strong word was needed to silence dissent. The night before we were due to board ship I called the team together. 'We're going to load up with luggage tonight, take it to the port, and put it on the ship,' I told them. 'And it's going to sail because God said it's going to sail.'

The next day, even as Elsa and I were going up the ramp with the last of the *olim*, a barge came up and filled the ship with fuel. On board we found a group of our intercessors. They had stood by us unshaken through this time, disregarding what they were seeing and hearing. I sat across from them at the table but couldn't speak. I just wept with relief. It had a tremendous effect on us all. We embraced and Elsa and I walked back down the ramp into the gathering darkness.

The second sailing was only a week away and we were dismayed to learn that there were even fewer *olim* registered than for the first. They had flocked to our trial sailings from all over the Soviet Union a year before. Many had been waiting years for the opportunity.

But the torrent of *aliyah* had now dwindled to a steady

stream of just one-third of the previous year's peak. There were also new border and custom controls which restricted *olim* and their belongings from entering Ukraine from other republics, and the Jewish Agency had put in place its own structure of direct flights. Instead of more bookings we got cancellations.

We saw that we must develop our own booking network. But as we began to contact the Jewish community, they were slow to respond and were reluctant to display our information. Many of the Jewish people of Ukraine still bore open wounds from their terrible suffering at the hands of Gentiles during the Holocaust.

During our first visit to Kiev, the capital, Elsa and I had visited the grassy park on the outskirts of the city called Babi Yar. A guide told us its story. When the German army came into Kiev in 1941 they announced to all the Jews, 'Get your belongings ready, you are being resettled.'

They were gathered in a huge crowd at Babi Yar. Each family left its money at a table. Their belongings were laid down in a pile. Then they were told to undress and were driven in groups of a hundred to the edge of a great ravine. A woman who gave birth at the site went with her newborn baby in her arms. As they approached the ravine the realization came over them that there would be no resettlement. They were mowed down by machine gun fire. Over 33,000 people died that day. Many were only injured and buried while still alive. Our guide told us that the earth was moving for days after the massacre.

Elsa and I were devastated. We walked silently back to the car. Neither of us could say anything.

We'd heard about this before. But somehow when we really saw with our own eyes – to know it happened **here** – we faced the evil and cruelty of mankind. It was a shock for us to accept, coming from our sheltered background.

Later Elsa and I went to an uncultivated field near the port in Odessa. It seemed no one wanted to build on it. A modest memorial stone explained why. In October 1941, six days after German and Romanian troops had occupied Odessa, an explosion blew up the Romanian command headquarters and killed the commanding general. As retribution, 19,000 Jews were assembled in a fenced-off area, sprayed with petrol and burned alive. The next day 16,000 more were marched in long columns to a nearby village. First they were machine-gunned in groups of 50 and then, to save time, locked in warehouses, which were then set ablaze. Panicked mothers attempting to throw their children from the windows were met with grenades and bullets.

'Where were you Christians when all this happened?' one Jewish leader asked when we said we'd come to help them go home. 'Nobody came in our time of need.'

Opposition from a source I'd never expected compounded this initial suspicion and mistrust. Instructions came to Jewish Agency field workers from headquarters in Jerusalem to steer *olim* away from our sailings. Families were warned that if they arrived in Haifa port with their belongings they would be stranded at the dock with no one to help them.

Finally advertisements appeared in the Ukrainian newspapers featuring a picture of a ship with a big red X over it. Underneath was the headline:

'THE SAILINGS FROM ODESSA TO HAIFA
ARE NOT TAKING PLACE.'

It was signed by the Jewish Agency.

I was shattered. I knew when I was going into the former Soviet Union I would have a battle on my hands. I didn't expect it with the Jews or within Israel. But then the Lord graciously reminded me that Moses had his hands full not only with the Egyptians, but also with his own people. Nothing had changed. Initially Agency officials had grave reservations that we Christians would have the ability to do this work. They feared we might disappear after a few months, leaving them to take over our responsibilities. Somehow it seemed they also saw our help as competition in a sphere which had until then been exclusively theirs.

We hit the low point on the fifth weekly sailing that left Odessa on Good Friday at the end of April. Three hundred and twenty beds were paid for, but only 10 *olim* were on the ship.

I came under severe attack. By now half our volunteers had left or been dismissed. Some men who had worked with us called a public meeting in London to ask me to justify why we were spending so much money for so few people. They doubted the vision and felt that I was unwise to charter such a big ship for weekly sailings.

I felt humiliated by the call for a public meeting. I asked myself where it would lead. Would I be exposed as one who had acted out of the flesh? Had I really heard the Lord? I felt that I had failed and for the first time began to think of giving up.

In the middle of the night I got out of bed in our room at the Odessa camp and lay on my stomach, nose down on the carpet, weeping. 'I can't take it any more,' I cried out to the Lord. A breaking up was going on, a breaking of my pride that I was the one chosen to do this work. It was painful, humbling.

I climbed back into bed, sobs still racking my body as I lay next to Elsa. She was awake and spoke to me in the darkened room. 'I want to tell you a story. There was a man who built the best ship ever. It took him 120 years. And there were only eight people on it.' I realized she was talking about Noah. It was an amazing revelation. It gave me courage. Elsa was marvellous. She never doubted one moment that the Lord had called us.

A few days later we flew to Jerusalem. The Jewish Agency now made an offer to pay us $180 for each immigrant we brought on our sailings! I was at first overjoyed and thought this might be our answer.

'Lord, what are you saying?' I asked. 'Do we accept or not?

Do we continue with the sailings or not?' Our team in Odessa came out against accepting the offer, but I still took over a week to consider. It offered a way of escape from the rising criticism. But finally the Lord did not allow me to accept. He reminded me that He has called the Gentiles to carry His sons and daughters back home.

The public meeting was held on *Tisha b'Av*, the day of disasters on the Jewish calendar. It was on this day Solomon's temple was destroyed by the Babylonians in 587 BC **and** the second temple by the Romans. With very mixed emotions of pain, indignation, and apprehension I flew to London with Elsa.

We walked into the meeting room in a hotel near Heathrow airport and found about 50 people there. Several of our faithful intercessors were on hand just to pray. I took a seat at a table at the front with Johannes Facius and Kjell Sjoberg. I saw other leaders of the Intercessory Prayer Conference who had flown in: Eliyahu Ben Haim from Israel and Robert Währer from Switzerland. Kingsley Priddy had come in from the Bible College of Wales. These men all knew me intimately and had been standing with us in prayer. All were recognized Christian leaders. Even the dissenters respected and accepted them.

The meeting was quite tense at the beginning. Johannes emerged as the chairman and together with Kjell defused the situation. They handled the discussion in the Spirit and with a sensitive, listening ear. All had the opportunity to speak from the heart. No one was steamrollered.

A few argued that we were wasting God's resources. I was astounded when the leaders completely dismissed the financial issue. 'The number of *olim* is not the issue,' Johannes said. 'We must look at the wider spiritual dimension.'

It became clear that the united opinion of the leadership was that the call we had was from the Lord and it was His will for the sailings to proceed. The leaders affirmed their willingness to share in the responsibility and from this the Ebenezer

Emergency Fund gained its international advisory board. Not all in the end rejoiced, but there was a sense of peace.

We stayed for a meal afterwards with friends. 'Am I glad this is over,' I sighed to Elsa. Only then I started to realize all of this had been from the Lord. It had been one of the most painful episodes of my life, but I saw God meant it for good. I no longer felt so important – this was really God's work and I was just one of His servants. He is in the business of making us into men and women He can use. As Elsa often reminded me, 'It's not what we do for the Lord which really counts, but what He is doing in us.'

Now for the first time I grasped that our prayer and action counted beyond the boundaries of Ebenezer's own operation. I wrote to our supporters:

> 'Out of these past three months the Lord has moved mightily in the heavenlies, laying the foundations of a work far greater than anyone of us can visualize. The Lord has shown us so clearly the intercessory nature of the project, that we do not just have the privilege of bringing out thousands of *olim*, but through overcoming, at every level, every opposition that hell can bring against the work, the Holy Spirit would gain a position of intercession for Jews worldwide to be brought home to Israel, according to God's word.'

Kingsley's experience with intercession helped bring this into focus for us. He was always keenly interested in our work and in a remarkable letter helped me also to see why I'd been led by the Holy Spirit to decline the underwriting of the Jewish Agency for Operation Exodus. The true intercessor, he wrote, becomes **personally responsible** for the object of his prayer:

> 'You see, Intercession is not prayer, nor even very intense prayer. Anyone may pray, and pray earnestly, for

something, and yet not be committed to be irrevocably responsible, at any cost, for its fulfilment. The intercessor is.

'In Intercession there is Identification with the matter or persons interceded for. The intercessor is willing to take the place of the one prayed for; to let **their** need become **his** need; to let **their** need be met at **his** expense and to let **their** suffering become the travail of **his** own heart.'

'That is how the Lord Jesus *"made intercession for the transgressors"* (Isaiah 53:12). *"He was numbered with the transgressors,"* and *"He was wounded for* (their) *transgressions"* (Isaiah 53:5). He had to be "identified" with sinners; He secured their pardon by vicariously paying the debt that they owed.'

(The full text of this letter is reprinted in Appendix 1).

To our surprise, the leading Israeli newspaper *Yediot Ahronot* had picked up on the crisis in Odessa. They sent a journalist to investigate and the same week as the Heathrow meeting published a multi-page spread in their weekend edition exposing what they called the Jewish Agency's efforts to 'torpedo' the sailings.

It was taken up in the Knesset. I was called to testify before a special session of the immigration committee. I came over from Odessa on a sailing the night before. I was sweating. To go to parliament! Somehow I was unable to prepare what to say.

That morning I entered the crowded meeting room and saw a high-powered team from the Jewish Agency, members of the Knesset, government officials and the news media. As the meeting began, Yasha Kedmi, who had years of experience with Soviet Jewry as head of the prime minister's Liaison Bureau, came out strongly behind us. He argued that the decision of many *olim* to come to Israel hinged on whether they could bring their possessions with them, which our sailings allowed. He also revealed that since 1989 his bureau had been calling for the opening of sea routes in case of emergencies when flights might be impossible.

I listened to a whispered translation of his comments from Hebrew:

> 'This group wants to finance the attempt of the state of Israel and of the Jewish people to bring *olim* by way of the sea. So why not agree and tell them, "Thank you"?'

I had given the committee members a paper listing some of the biblical references undergirding our work. Knesset member Avraham Ravitz, an Orthodox rabbi with full beard and black clothing, interrupted the meeting to ask for a Hebrew Bible, then turned and addressed me for the first time. 'In your paper you brought a quotation from Jeremiah 16, which is a correct and lovely verse. I want to direct our attention to what is said at the end of the chapter:

> *"O LORD, my strength and my fortress,*
> *My refuge in the day of affliction,*
> *The Gentiles shall come to You*
> *From the ends of the earth and say,*
> *'Surely our fathers have inherited lies,*
> *Worthlessness and unprofitable things.'*
> *Will a man make gods for himself,*
> *Which are not gods?"*
>
> Jeremiah 16:19–20

'I will tell you why I raise these verses. On the sailing two years ago – and I don't know if this was your organization – matters were not so smooth from the standpoint of the Christian group's attempt to influence the *olim*. I'm speaking with you in the most open manner, as one religious man to another.

'Truly Jews should be brought to Israel at any price, but not at the price of an attempt to influence them to receive a different religion. I do not agree to this price ... We must remember we are dealing with *olim* who were cut off from the religion of their fathers for 73 years, and they are coming here to return to their roots. And *oy vavoy* to us if they will be influenced by a group of missionaries on their way to the country ... We need to strictly guard the Jews making their way to the Holy Land, to the land of their fathers and to the religion of their fathers, to the land of the *Tanakh* which is promised to them by the Holy One, Blessed be He, so they will not be confused.'

I knew I had to speak up. 'Mr Chairman, I'm surprised to find myself in the Knesset. I'm a simple guy who serves an extraordinary God. And I know that the God of Israel called me to serve and to carry home the children of Israel, the chosen people.

'I want to say in the clearest possible way that my hands are clean and my motives are pure. All of the volunteers working with us pledge that they have no missionary intentions and they will not engage in missionary activity.'

At this point I also pulled out my Bible. 'Listen, this book is written by you. If you read your own Bible it says in Isaiah that the Gentiles should carry your sons and daughters back. I want you to know that all over the world there are Christians who have committed themselves to bringing the Jewish people home.

'During the last two-and-a-half years I spent more time in Odessa than any other place, and I have travelled extensively throughout the former Soviet Union. And I understand that the situation is deteriorating. We are living on borrowed time. We need to do all that we can to bring these *olim* home as quickly as possible.

'I think it is very important that there will be an additional escape route beyond what is now established. In chapter 60, verse 9 of Isaiah it says explicitly that they will come home by ship, that *"the ships of Tarshish will bring your sons from afar."*

Rabbi Ravitz was following along in his Hebrew Bible. 'And it is also written there,' he interjected, '"*that their silver and their property is with them.*" That is to say, their baggage is with them. Isn't that what we've been talking about here?'

From that point he and the rest of the committee were behind us. And without my speaking a word about the Jewish Agency, that which was covered was revealed and the hidden things made known. 'The Agency was wrong all the way,' Uri Gordon, head of its immigration department, told the committee. He showed them telegrams sent to Agency representatives instructing them to begin helping us.

'We call on the Jewish Agency to settle this matter at the earliest possible time,' concluded the chairman, Emanuel Zisman, at the end of the hearing. 'We recommend that this be given the highest priority ... because you see this involves a real danger of loss of life.'

Afterwards the rabbi came and shook hands with me and said, 'Now I feel more comfortable about your helping our people to come home.' He said I had spoken well. Not me! The Lord had taken me by His hand.

Uri Gordon wrote us that week, 'to extend our appreciation to your sponsors. You are part of a great historic event, the ingathering of the Jewish people to their land'.

At the Odessa base a new atmosphere was blooming. We rebuilt our team of volunteers, drawing on some 20 nations, and there was real joy among them. They were united in their love for the Lord and His word. Even after tiring hard work they could sing and dance to Him. The *olim* could see them shining with the love of the Lord.

A German couple, Hinrich and Elke, took over the leadership of the team and brought strength and commitment. Hinrich had been managing the construction of a huge power plant when he applied to join us months earlier. Our invitation arrived the day he finished the project. He immediately took leave of absence to join us.

At the camp he recounted for us a conversation with his employer at the celebration of the plant's completion. 'Why are you going to help the Jews?' he asked Hinrich. 'We know that young girls are romantic and old ladies pray, but why you?'

'God said to Abraham, "I will bless those who bless you,"' Hinrich replied. 'I'm not afraid to ruin my career. You'll promote me while I'm away.' His boss recalled that remark when he phoned Hinrich months later in Odessa with news of promotion!

Hinrich's father was an officer in the German army fighting in the Soviet Union until he was severely wounded a second time in the Ukraine in 1943. He knew about the Jews being massacred and told Hinrich about the inner turmoil between his conscience and his oath of allegiance. He very deeply embedded in Hinrich's heart that the Holocaust must not happen again. As we met with the *olim* in the camp's dining hall for a farewell evening before each sailing, Hinrich read to them the prophecy of Isaiah 60:14: *'Also the sons of those who afflicted you shall come bowing to you.'*

And we really embraced the Ukrainians on the camp staff, treating them as human beings, with a smile. It was new for them. Under the Communist system they had worked under fear and the pressure of the boss. Now for the first time each was respected as a person. Gradually we broke the spirit of the camp. A big *babushka* (grandmother) in the kitchen insisted on kissing me whenever she saw me.

We had an evening together with the staff and gave them Russian Bibles and children's Bibles. Most took the children's Bibles, which were illustrated and easier to understand. 'Look, this is a book written thousands of years ago,' I told them. 'We live in a time when what is written by these men of old, these prophets, is taking place. You are a privileged person to have a part in this.'

One grey-haired man on the staff always looked drunk. He came to me the day after our meeting. 'I couldn't drink last night,' he said through a translator. 'I was reading the Bible the whole time.' When we gave them the Bible they treated it with far greater respect than in the West. This had been a forbidden book for 70 years. They realized we were putting something very special into their hands.

Then came perhaps the most amazing development of all. Israel's only television channel had sent a crew to Odessa to prepare a documentary on our work. The night that the stunning news first broke of the Rabin-Arafat accord, all Israel gathered before the television screen for the details. Then the newscaster said, 'We have one more report, that belongs perhaps to a different rhythm, that of God – but it too has good news and hope for the future.'

With that the programme switched to strains of our volunteers singing 'He Has Made Me Glad' in the Odessa camp. There followed a remarkable 14 minutes guiding the Israeli people through our whole operation, from picking up *olim* at the railway station to bringing them to the port of Haifa. There were interviews with several volunteers, but the focus of the programme was on action more than words. Before the eyes of the nation passed scenes of service and love: volunteers from all the earth carrying the immigrants' baggage, dancing with their children, waving and singing farewell at dockside. Lingering close-ups searched the volunteers' faces. One could almost hear the questions being asked: Who are these people? Why are they doing this for us?

From the seeming death of the Good Friday sailing the Holy Spirit had brought resurrection. Operation Exodus had shown the entire nation God's love and faithfulness to His Word.

During these weeks the number of *olim* on each sailing had been steadily rising. The name of Ebenezer was becoming well known and the Jewish community started to accept and trust us. For the 25th and final sailing of the year our volunteers picked up 22 different groups of *olim* at the train station, plus others brought in by bus from outlying villages. The camp was fully booked and we were forced to open a second. We faced a new and welcome crisis: would we have enough beds on board ship?

In the end all were able to embark. Some volunteers slept on cabin floors. 'Tonight my heart is full of thanks,' I told them after Elsa and I boarded. 'God has answered my prayers.'

As we were going under the bridges of Istanbul I was standing near a handicapped immigrant who was using a pair of binoculars. 'May I borrow those for a moment?' I asked him. I wanted to study the old stone fortresses on the shore. He handed them to me, but when I went to return them he refused.

'No, no – they are yours,' he told me. 'I want you to keep them. You have done so much for my people.' I was deeply moved. They were probably his most prized possession.

The evening before docking in Haifa we savoured more of the sweet aroma of reconciliation as we shared an evening with the *olim*. How they cheered when I told them the story of the removal of the BLASCO president earlier that year!

'We are so used to that attitude,' one woman explained. 'Someone not liking us simply because we are Jews.' They were amazed to think that God would intervene in response to prayer.

'I just want to praise the God of Israel for all His help,' I told them. 'You need to learn to pray yourselves in Israel and God will help you with your problems.'

The love of God filled the room like a cloud as our volunteers came and shared their hearts with the *olim*. Afterwards I saw an American named Becky exchanging tears and hugs with a greying, bent immigrant called Rebekah. 'We're working together as one,' Rebekah told us. 'I've never felt such personal attention and love.'

An older man who looked like a former officer in the Red Army came to me, shook my hand, and said, 'Once I was a communist. But now I believe in God, seeing the love shown to us by your people.'

Also with us was Joseph, a Holocaust survivor. We had invited him and other survivors to travel on the ship for a once-in-a-lifetime tour of Israel, even though they did not plan to emigrate. 'We are very surprised and totally amazed,' he said after the meeting. 'We were really crying. We couldn't believe it was true.'

He shared with us his story from the war years:

> 'My family and I, together with all the Jews, were gathered by the Germans. With my mother and sister, my grandfather and brother, we walked 35 kilometres to a camp. It was very cold; many died on the way. The camp was called the "place of death". Those who entered it didn't leave. We lived in terrible conditions. My mother and sister died there.
>
> 'Before the war we had a Russian woman living and working in our home. She did the best she could for us. She followed us to the camp. She tried to pass food to us. After the camp was liberated by the Russian army she took my older brother and me and helped us to find our father. She was a real Christian, the most precious person I've met in my life. She took the role of saviour in our family. We wouldn't have survived without her.'

For Elsa and me it was like a ray of sunshine to hear from time to time of these Christians who risked their lives to save Jews during the Holocaust. Such help was forbidden by the German occupying forces on pain of death. We remembered others –

the Jews called them 'righteous Gentiles' – like Corrie ten Boom, whose family hid Jews in their home in occupied Holland. When arrested she and her sister were taken in a cattle car together with Jews to a concentration camp. Only Corrie survived. These were true intercessors – standing with the Jews even to the point of death.

The director of the Department for the Righteous at the Yad Vashem Holocaust memorial and museum in Jerusalem, Dr Mordecai Paldiel, reported that a majority of the hundreds of rescuers he's studied were motivated by their Christian faith. The Church as an institution came out of the Holocaust besmirched, in his view, by its failure to take a stand. 'But the small persons had a better grasp of what Christianity was than the hierarchy,' he said. 'As a religion of faith, love, and brotherhood, Christianity has shown itself capable of being a very potent force ... The Sermon on the Mount, the Good Samaritan – they were moved by it. It speaks in favour of the teachings of Christianity.'

CHAPTER 7

Flight of Faith

'"Hear the word of the Lord, O nations,
And declare it in the isles afar off, and say,
'He who scattered Israel will gather him,
And keep him as a shepherd does his flock.'"'

Jeremiah 31:10

We had only just cleared all the bills from the sailings when Esther turned up in my Bournemouth office. Her head of white hair didn't fool me. This widow and former headmistress had been a strong and determined volunteer with us through the difficult months in Odessa. And rather than return to England's quiet shores after the last sailing, she and another Englishwoman set off in the thick of winter for the former Soviet republic of Armenia. Esther had heard of severe conditions there and went to investigate the state of the Jewish community.

They met some Armenian Jews, struggling to live with the effects of the massive 1988 earthquake and ongoing warfare with Azerbaijan. Electricity came on for just one or two hours a day and nobody knew when. Fresh water only came every three days.

'Do you want to go to Israel?' Esther asked a Jewish community leader in the capital, Yerevan.

'There are no flights to Israel from our country,' he replied. 'The only way is to first go all the way to Moscow and we don't have the money for that.'

'What if we brought a plane?' Esther persisted. The leader shrugged sceptically.

Esther and her friend promised to return. In England they gathered aid and flew back into Armenia in February with many boxes of supplies for the Jewish people. The community was stunned. The women had kept their word. No one had fulfilled promises before.

'Is there **really** any possibility you'd get us on a plane to fly to Israel?' the leader asked.

'Well … yes,' Esther said, thinking, 'I don't know who will pay!'

Returning to England they went to an aircraft charter company and booked a plane for a London/Yerevan/Tel Aviv/London circuit three months hence. They had no money. Esther had only a pension. Her friend owned a home. They came out of the charter company office, stood on the pavement and looked at each other. 'What have we done?' Esther said. 'We've booked a plane that will cost £60,000!'

That's when she came to me. 'We know we're not to collect money for the plane,' Esther said with quiet certainty. She was always sensitive to the instruction of the Holy Spirit. 'We can collect humanitarian aid in England to **bring** on the plane, but God is going to pay for the plane.'

At the end of her report Esther smiled. 'Would you pray about whether Ebenezer should be involved?'

'You know, you're always costing me a lot of money,' I teased her as I thought over our situation. There had been a period of extensive prayer and waiting before we covered the sailing bills and I felt no inclination to branch out into an unknown republic. 'I would need a clear sign from the Lord to know if we should get involved in this.'

Elsa and I started to pray, and didn't seem to get any answer. Week after week I would get a phone call from Esther, looking for one. 'I've heard nothing from the Lord,' I told her. 'This has nothing to do with me.'

I felt for her deeply after my own experiences. But much as I enquired of the Lord about our involvement, there was only silence. I knew I had no choice but to stand still and to continue waiting on Him. 'We know that the Lord God of Israel has the whole situation in hand,' I faxed Esther, who was now organizing the Jewish people in Yerevan. 'We feel He will make a way of escape and should we receive a direct signal you will, of course, be the first to know.'

Finally, Esther's colleague phoned at 11 a.m. one day and said, 'Unless we pay today the flight will be cancelled and it will do tremendous harm because we have gathered humanitarian aid and, more importantly, Jews to fly out.' She asked for a loan and was willing to sell her house to repay it.

'I'll give you my reply by 3 p.m.,' I told her, and called a few trusted intercessors and Elsa and asked them to urgently seek the Lord's guidance. It was, in fact, Elsa who came back first. She had felt a prompting to look up Scriptures which spoke of lending and came to Luke 11:5–8, the friend asking to borrow three loaves at midnight.

'They are really desperate,' she told me. 'It is nearly midnight for the flight. And they have been knocking for all these weeks.' The amazing thing was that a Swedish intercessor then faxed me the same words. I knew the Lord was saying it was right – and phoned back to say we'd cover the cost as a three-month loan.

Only later did Elsa share with me the other Scripture she had found: 'When you loan, do not expect to be paid back!'

So I established direct contact with the air charter company and satisfied myself that we had a proper contract. They were experienced in such mercy flights. I packed my suitcase. I was sure I'd be on the plane. But somehow the Lord didn't give me the green light to go. I had no peace about it. It was disappointing – I could not understand.

On flight day I asked the company to keep us posted. The first report was everything okay, but hours later they called to say they had no landing permission at Ben Gurion airport. 'What do you mean, you have no landing permission?' I questioned. 'You should have applied long before this!'

I soon realized that permission had, in fact, been denied. The Israeli aviation authorities had checked with the Jewish Agency, which cast doubt on the operation by saying there were few if any Jews in Armenia! I was taken aback. The aircraft was already in the air.

I sent an urgent fax to the Israeli ambassador in Moscow, whose consuls had approved the documents of all these Jews: 'You issued the visas, now permission to enter the country is needed.' No answer was forthcoming. Hours went by.

Esther phoned to tell me the plane had landed and the aid was unloaded. Then the phone line to Armenia went dead. Our efforts to call all afternoon were in vain. I drew up a contingency plan to take the plane into Cyprus and put the *olim* on the overnight ferry to Haifa. Finally, about 10 p.m., came a call from the air charter company confirming, much to my relief, that Israel had granted landing permission. Now I understood that the Lord had kept me back from the flight to manage this crisis.

But in Yerevan Esther found that after unloading the plane the authorities wouldn't let it depart. They demanded a fee of $9,000 rather than the $500 previously agreed. Esther spent the entire day trying to negotiate without success, meeting people, running up and down stairs. There was nothing to eat or drink at the airport. Around midnight the power was out and she was going up the stairs in the dark. She went to a corner and felt as if arrows were coming at her from every direction.

'Have we been two foolish women, Lord?' she cried out. 'Doing something presumptuous, not from you? All these Jews down here with no homes, and no money to pay for the plane. We don't have $9,000 to get them to Israel. What are we going to do?'

She felt as if something like a shaft of light hit her, and all she heard was 'Get the money.' She thought, 'Get the money? Then it must be here somewhere!' and ran back to her friend. They pooled their resources and turned to a pastor friend. He brought all the money he had: $1,500 given to help buy an office for his church. All together they came up with $3,000.

Esther prayed, 'Lord, where are we going to get the other $6,000 from?' 'Go to the pilots,' came the thought. She and her friend ran over the pitch-black airfield to find the plane. There were the pilots and crew, sitting in the dark waiting for news. Esther told them what had happened.

'How much do you need?' the captain asked.

'Six thousand dollars,' she said.

He looked at them in amazement. He put his hand in his pocket and brought out a wad of banknotes. 'I think you'll find $6,000 here,' he said. 'You can borrow it and pay it back when you can.' As he was getting dressed for the flight he had seen his savings sitting on the cupboard. On impulse he stuffed the money in his pocket. It was the exact amount needed! Many hours later the plane landed at Ben Gurion airport, carrying 67 *olim*.

Esther remained in Yerevan, where she and her partner were praying about the finances to repay Ebenezer for the flight. She told me she saw a picture in her mind of an invoice which said, 'Paid in full.' Minutes later the phone rang. It was my fax, sharing with them the second Scripture Elsa had given. God had released us to pay for the plane.

Esther wasn't finished. A plea came for help from Jewish people in Nagorno-Karabakh, the Armenian enclave and scene of fierce fighting between Armenia and Azerbaijan for control of it. Esther set off in a private car to investigate with Vlasta, a Czech volunteer. Bagrat, from the church in Yerevan, was driving. As they climbed the serpentine road into the mountains snow began to fall, more heavily the higher they got. They neared the peak and were stopped behind several

lorries parked on the steep incline, unable to continue because
of ice on the road. Vlasta tells the rest of the story:

> 'I was in the front seat with a thermos in one hand, a cup
> in the other, enjoying some coffee, laughing and talking.
> Suddenly I realized the lorry about ten metres in front of
> us was starting to slide back. I didn't understand what was
> happening. Then I saw the driver and a passenger jump
> out and I realized the problem was serious. I didn't know
> what to do. I dropped the coffee and tried to open the
> door,' she told me, demonstrating with frantic hand
> gestures.
>
> 'It was my first time in the front and I couldn't get the
> door open. I realized it was too late. I closed my eyes and
> I said, "Jesus – help!" When I opened my eyes I saw the
> lorry stopped one metre away from us. The lorry driver
> was shaking when they brought him back a half-hour
> later. "I had said goodbye to you and the lorry already," he
> told us, "because a situation like this always ends up as a
> great catastrophe."
>
> 'We knew that God was with us and we should
> continue.' They went on to help two Jewish families
> come out of the enclave, where many people had been
> killed and maimed. I have been amazed at the lengths to
> which the Holy Spirit would take our volunteers on
> behalf of the Jewish people – even at risk of their lives –
> and I am so thankful that all have returned well from their
> journeys.

The pioneering work in Armenia proved that there were
indeed Jewish people there who wanted to come to Israel. The
Jewish Agency agreed to finance a second flight of 98 *olim*
organized by Esther and her friend, and Ebenezer then
sponsored a third with 115 *olim* in December 1994.

I was there to meet this flight in Tel Aviv. Passengers

straggled in, the men unshaven, tired but exhilarated. Elsa and I had visited Armenia the month before and I recognized many of the *olim*. There was such joy. It was a very emotional coming together. Many had tears in their eyes.

A highway had been blazed for the ancient Jewish community of this isolated country! We turned the work in Armenia over to members of the local church. They sent a steady stream of *olim* out to Odessa by air, where they joined sailings of the *Dmitry Shostakovich*, which we renewed in 1995. By this point over 500 Jews had come out of Armenia – after we'd first been told there were none there! And when Bagrat uncovered an old Armenian telephone directory – which are few and far between in the former Soviet Union – he found over 1,500 families with Jewish names to contact. I have no doubt there are far more Jews hidden away in the former Soviet Union than the official statistics tell us. God knows His people. He will find them.

Elsa and I planned to return to Armenia. We were in Moscow and the Israeli consul there was taken aback when I said, 'Tomorrow we fly to Armenia.'

'Are you sure?' he asked me. 'There is unrest there! I advise you not to go.'

Elections had just been held which many Armenians believed were fraudulent. Riot police used tear gas, water cannons and shots in the air to drive back a crowd threatening to storm the parliament. But we made contact with a church in Armenia and learned they had obtained permission to hold a conference about Israel at which I was invited to speak. Elsa and I prayed and felt we should go.

Soldiers and tanks were everywhere. We had no visas, but even the immigration officers made us feel welcome. We had a most marvellous time. The 320 seats were packed for the day-long conference, with a few standing at the back. I asked how long I could speak. The pastor looked surprised and said, 'As long as you like.'

It was a dynamic meeting. They wanted to know more about Israel. When I shared about our work they spontaneously took up a collection. Then at night, to close the conference, the senior pastor took the microphone. 'Now we will bless Gustav and Elsa.' They took up a love offering for us. I had tears in my eyes when I saw those who had nothing coming forward to give us money, pencils, rings, chocolates – whatever they had. Truly the Lord richly rewarded our obedience to go there.

In almost every church we have been privileged to visit in the former Soviet Union the pastor has readily given over the pulpit for me to give a teaching on Israel and to share the vision of Operation Exodus. They understand the Jewish people – like them they have suffered much and so are willing to help. We even have some of these churches giving us a tithe of their meagre income.

It has been a double blessing for Elsa and me every time we have found a church in the West whose pastor has taught his congregation God's end-time purposes for the people and land of Israel. But more often when I share silence falls over a congregation. They are not quite sure how to respond. Some say, 'We have never heard anything like that.' So I always endeavour to work with much Scripture, as in this way our own eyes were first opened to the place of Israel.

I was invited to speak at a mid-week meeting in a Lutheran church in Germany. After I shared the vision of Operation Exodus the pastor, in casual dress, came forward. I thought he would pray and dismiss the congregation. I was not a little surprised when he said with conviction, 'I have listened carefully, and feel I should say that what Mr Scheller shared was fulfilled when the Jews returned from Babylon. It is no longer a subject for our times.' It was quite an occasion for me, standing there in front of the congregation. I listened and said nothing. Years ago I would have argued. Unlike the limited return of the Jews from Babylon, this return is to be global and permanent, as portrayed, for example, in Ezekiel 37:21–28. But I have learned to let God be the one who justifies.

During a time of prayer and fasting the Lord showed me that *aliyah* could be compared with the parable of the prodigal son in Luke 15. The Jewish people in the land of the north are coming under increasing pressure: economic pressure, political pressure, anti-Semitism. They suffer! Like the prodigal son they realize it is better for them to go home.

And then God showed me His Father's heart. It is a broken heart. I saw it so clearly; He is longing for His people to come home. He is on the look-out and says, 'Come My children, come now.'

And then He showed me the elder brother. We, the Body of Christ, are the elder brother! Because the overwhelming majority of Christians do not care about God's chosen people and what is happening with Israel. The Father is grieving over the attitude of the elder brother.

Many in the Church know that the Great Commission must be completed before the return of the Lord (Matthew 24:14). But if we do not also recognize the role of Israel as we enter the end times we are only standing on one leg. We see from Acts 1:6 and 3:21 that Jesus will come when the kingdom is restored to Israel, to reign '*upon the throne of David and over His kingdom*' (Isaiah 9:7).

As I've been praying I feel the Lord is saying to me, 'Gustav, I have waited almost two thousand years for this time.' Now is the time. God in His infinite mercy has given us this glorious opportunity to help His chosen people return to the Promised Land. I believe with all my heart that our actions are recorded in Heaven and will bring joy and happiness to the Father.

CHAPTER 8

To the Ends of the Earth

'Proclaim, give praise, and say,
"O Lord, save your people,
The remnant of Israel!"
Behold, I will bring them from the north country,
and gather them from the ends of the earth.'

Jeremiah 31:7–8

Maria, one of our team members, had been speaking to me for some time about the Jewish people in yet another former Soviet republic, Kazakhstan. 'I don't want to know about Kazakhstan,' I told her. 'First we have to consolidate our existing work.' It is a huge country, bigger than all of Western Europe, and predominantly Muslim. But Maria continued to nudge me about Ebenezer's involvement. Reluctantly, I decided one day to add it to my prayer diary. As I was making the entry I was not a little surprised to see it was on the day we were called to pray for this very nation.

Early in 1995 Elsa and I flew into the city of Karaganda, in the centre of Kazakhstan, in a propeller-driven Aeroflot aircraft. The hostess brought drinks. It was only water, in a not-very-appetizing plastic mug, which was then rinsed and re-used for the other passengers. Strangely, food and drink do not seem to have the same importance to us as in the West. When we are on the Lord's assignments we are consumed with our task.

We joyfully accept food and living conditions that we would never put up with back home.

I must confess we sometimes call this company not Aeroflot, but 'Aeroflop.' As a frequent traveller with this airline, I could add many pages to this book sharing some of our eventful flight experiences. To sum up: flight delays, cancellation of actual flights and even closure of whole airports due to lack of fuel or weather conditions. None of these are unusual. Often there are extra passengers standing for the entire flight as paying guests of the captain! I jokingly enquire of my wife whether she has packed our screwdriver. We cover each flight in prayer, knowing that when we are in the perfect will of the Father there is no safer place for us on all the earth, even on an 'Aeroflop' plane.

As we stepped out of the aircraft in Karaganda, waiting for us on the tarmac was the leader of the Jewish community, Leonid, who later became a dear and trusted friend and a loyal representative of Ebenezer. At the end of our visit Leonid embraced me warmly, and said, 'One day my grandchildren will know that Gustav has come to Karaganda to call the Jews home to Israel.'

Through our visits we have seen firsthand the survival battle of the people living in this harsh land. Doctors, teachers and pensioners had not been paid for six to eight months. The infrastructure was collapsing – the electricity and water supplies were cut; there had been no cooking gas in the homes for a year and in severe weather conditions many homes and offices had no heating. By now many of the Jewish people had realized it was time to leave. The Lord used this strong bond of friendship in the following year to bring out 1,000 *olim* from that mountainous land.

I can still see the face of a Jewish lady in her early 50s who had adopted three street children. She looked hopefully to me and said, 'I want to go home – but only if I can take these children with me.' For a fleeting moment I thought such a desire to be impossible. She had no documents. She had picked up these little children off the street and did not even know their full names. How would it be possible to secure Israeli visas in such circumstances?

It was many months later when our representative telephoned me and told me that this lady and her children would be on our next flight. Tears welled up in my eyes. God had again made the impossible possible.

During those months the shipping line continued to flourish, and when I was due to fly out to Odessa for the last sailing of 1995 I knew that I'd be put under extreme pressure. Our volunteers, Israeli shipping partners, the owners of the *Dmitry Shostakovich* and the owners of the transit camp in Odessa were all asking me, 'When will we sail again?'

But every time I inquired of the Lord I just couldn't get an answer. The night before I cried out to the Lord, 'Give me a clear sign what to do!'

Elsa and I had to leave the next morning at 4:00 a.m. for Heathrow airport. When I awoke, to my amazement my otherwise reliable Swiss watch had come to a standstill – and my morning reading in *Daily Watchwords* was, '*Stand still and see the salvation of the LORD.*' I knew God had spoken and it was no longer a problem for me. Some were disappointed, but I just knew we had to wait. I do not dare make a move until the time the Lord gives the revelation. If I go against what He has shown me my life is not worth living.

At the same time we found that we did not have sufficient funds to pay the final sailing bill. God had always provided through the years chiefly by the small gifts of faithful believers, but now we came under increasing pressure. Elsa and I were considering selling our Swiss apartment, which we had bought some years earlier for our retirement and had paid for over a period of 20 years. Elsa, being a wise woman, said, 'Let's fast and pray for a week.'

I will never forget that after five days of fasting an excited

Beverley telephoned me to say that Ebenezer had received a
substantial legacy, which would completely clear all our debts.
We were overjoyed. It was as if the Lord gave us back our
lovely apartment. Somehow I was reminded of Abraham,
who put Isaac on the altar and God abundantly blessed him for
it.

Then in early January I had the release that we would sail
again and I could start my negotiations. 'Lord,' I prayed one
morning at home, 'should we use the same vessel?' I jumped in
my car to drive to the office and switched on the radio. Usually
I listen to worship tapes, but I enjoyed the particular piece of
classical music that was playing. The announcer came on and
said, 'That was by Dmitry Shostakovich,' the Russian composer
for whom the ship was named! I knew the Lord was saying we
were to move ahead.

He knows the end from the beginning. On our return to
Odessa we found that mighty BLASCO was now in such
financial difficulty it had started to dispose of some of its
passenger fleet. This created competition and the new owners
of these vessels were eager to do business with us. We were
able to charter the *Dmitry Shostakovich* in 1996 on terms that
saved money and made our lives easier than if we'd accepted
the contract offered in December.

Even though we were now established in three republics I
found my heart was still stirring with an impression: 'Go where
no one else is going.' I knew that operations in difficult areas
wouldn't bring back the majority of *olim* to Israel. But I began
to see that Operation Exodus, as Johannes once put it, is more
than anything else a prophetic sign. Our calling is to open the
way like a plough and bring back the most impossible cases.

I thought I'd test the waters when I saw the senior official
for immigration at the Israeli embassy in Moscow. 'In which

part of the former Soviet Union do Jews most need help to make *aliyah*?' I asked him.

'Siberia,' he answered without any hesitation. It struck a chord in my heart. A few weeks later I was at the Israeli embassy in Kiev, asked the same question and instantly received the same reply.

I well remember the first time Elsa and I visited Siberia. Following the *Mediterranean Sky* sailings, the Lord had led us to explore many parts of the former Soviet Union and we travelled right across Russia on the trans-Siberian railway.

On the first leg of our journey we sat on the hard wooden benches of an old second-class carriage from Riga to Minsk. It was approaching midnight and, forgive the expression, my bottom hurt a bit by that time. I was tired, and I looked at Elsa. And as I looked at my wife I started laughing. I couldn't stop it. I looked at her and she giggled as well. After a while I said, 'Either we are utterly mad or this is the Lord.'

Finally we arrived at our hotel in Minsk. I had already gone to bed when the Lord reminded me that I hadn't done my evening reading. So I sat up, turned on the light and read that day's selection from 1 Corinthians 1:27:

> *'But God has chosen the foolish things of the world to put to shame the wise. And God has chosen the weak things of this world to put to shame the things which are mighty.'*

It made me feel good!

We spent eight days and nights on trains. It was bumpy. We couldn't read because the book would be shaking too much. It was best just to look out of the window. There was nothing to eat; we'd buy food when we stopped at a station for 15 minutes. When I stepped off the train I was never sure whether the platform was going up and down or if it was me! Poorly dressed women would stand there with whatever they had to sell. I remember one woman selling mashed potatoes from a pot in her baby's pushchair. I caught her eye and saw desperation.

During this journey Elsa and I made a side trip to see the Jewish autonomous region created by Stalin back in 1928. He moved Jews to the far end of Siberia, on the border with China – the middle of nowhere. We felt led to go there and visit the capital, Birobidzhan. It was quite an experience to pull into the train station and see the name of the city written in both Russian and Hebrew!

When we got there we had three addresses, possible contacts. At the first two places we couldn't find anybody. We went to the third one and met the leader of the entire Jewish community of the area. I shared my heart with him. He asked us to stay for a beautiful meal, and then he said, 'Tonight we are celebrating *Shavuot* at the synagogue. It will be packed. Will you come with us?' It was God's timing. The Lord had sent us all the way to the far end of Siberia exactly on that night when they would celebrate, when their little wooden synagogue would be full. And I had liberty that night to tell them, 'Now is the time to go home.'

We neared the end of our journey and were looking forward to flying to Japan the next day. Elsa and I must have spent about 200 hours on the train. Very often they played hard rock music in the coaches. It is good for headaches! Suddenly the rock music went quiet. Then, in the last few minutes, they started to play Handel's beautiful 'Hallelujah Chorus'. We'd never heard anything like that. In the middle of Siberia, at the far end of the earth! It was as if the Lord was saying, 'Well done, my good and faithful servants.' We were in tears. It was such a beautiful experience.

Three years later Elsa and I flew into Magadan, Russia's most far easterly city, to begin our work in earnest. The territory is so vast – three times the size of the US continent – that our flight from Moscow lasted eight hours. Stalin sent millions to prison camps at Magadan precisely for its isolation. It is accessible only by air, boat or, in season, a four-wheel drive vehicle carrying its own fuel supply along dirt roads and on ferries. No walls or guards were needed here – there was nowhere to flee.

Countless millions perished in the Siberian *gulag*. Many of these were Jews and Christians banished there for practicing their faith. For me this is the place nearest to hell on earth. And as Elsa and I looked at the run-down shacks and rubbish lying about we could sense a depression, like a spirit of death that still hovered over the area.

We felt prompted in our spirits to go on a prayer walk through parts of the city. We set out on a cold summer day. Patches of snow were still on the nearby mountain tops. We came to a high point directly overlooking the harbour, where ships had brought in the prisoners destined to die. It just gripped me and I had such a sense that the Lord was saying, 'Prophesy over this city.'

It was something I had never done. As we stood there Ezekiel's vision of dry bones came to me. I opened my Bible to Ezekiel 37:12 and spoke out the words:

> 'Thus says the Lord GOD: "Behold, O My people, I will open your graves and cause you to come up from your graves, and bring you into the land of Israel."'

I was deeply stirred. Tears came to my eyes. I just knew at that moment that the Lord was calling us to call forth his sons and daughters from the ends of the earth.

Elsa and I were invited to dinner in Magadan with a Jewish woman, her son and his young wife. This family had so little, but the mother worked for two days to prepare a beautiful meal. She put mountains of food on the table. We felt embarrassed. It was much more than we could eat. After the meal, as our hostess poured us steaming sweet tea, I pulled out my weapon, the Bible. 'Look what Moses said 3,000 years ago,' I told them, turning to Deuteronomy 30:4:

> *'If any of you are driven out to the farthest parts under heaven, from there the LORD your God will gather you.'*

I paused and looked them in the eyes. 'You live in the farthest part of the earth and it is time to go home.'

I'll never forget I was in Odessa for our first sailing of 1996 and the son and his wife turned up! 'You know,' he told me, 'when you spoke about going home to Israel I knew it was time.' They sold everything and flew to Moscow to have their papers approved by the Israeli embassy. But their plane broke down; they were left to walk long hours through the snow; they were attacked and robbed of all their money; even some of their belongings were stolen on the train to Odessa. By the time we met them they were devastated. But our people just loved them. When I said goodbye to them as they left to board the ship there was new hope.

We put together a team to 'fish' for more families like this one and help them with a safe, reliable route to Israel. We met in early 1996 in Khabarovsk, the capital of eastern Siberia, for a week of prayer and discussion, a time of mapping out our strategic plans. Our volunteers were to fan out from there in twos to spy out the land, pray and prophetically call forth the Jewish people.

The day before they were to leave I was privileged to speak at the local Bible school and shared that we were sending out fishing teams. There were students attending who had come from the various regions. A young man came forward. 'I can help your people to find the Jews in my city.' Others followed his lead. I could see the relief on the faces of our volunteers, who otherwise would have journeyed to these distant places not knowing a soul. This is not Europe or the United States. This is the end of the earth where communication is often complicated or even non-existent, and foreigners are watched with suspicion.

The students immediately made contact with their home churches and all our volunteers were met on their arrival and provided with food and a bed. Truly the Lord is the best administrator! Rarely have I felt His presence and love so much as out in that forsaken land.

Our volunteers returned with glorious stories of how God cares and makes a way to reach these isolated Jews. Yveta, a Czech girl who with her friend Martina was a pioneer of our work in Siberia, told of her visit to a remote settlement:

'I had a prompting. The Lord told me to leave Magadan and go into the interior. I wanted to visit a settlement 600 kilometres north. There is a minibus service, a weekly one that goes high into the interior only on dirt roads. When you drive there it is so unreal. You hold on because everything shakes all the time. The roads are full of holes.

'We were about 300 kilometres inland when the minibus broke down. When we opened the door hundreds of big mosquitoes came in and they were really hungry. I had never seen so many and such big mosquitoes in my life. The driver shook his head and said that he couldn't repair the vehicle. I knew we would be stranded for days before anyone found us. I prayed to the Lord, "Will You make a way?"

'Suddenly the driver looked up and said, "I have an idea." Within half an hour we drove on. When we got to the settlement it was like a miracle, an oasis in the middle of nowhere. There was a church and through them I found more than 30 Jewish families. Some of them had never heard anything like it when I came and said, "It's time to go home. The God of Israel, His plans for you are good. You have a future." They knew about Israel but didn't see how they could ever make it there. We told them we would help them.

'Some were so surprised that we could find them, because they never told anybody they were Jewish and thought nobody in the settlement knew – but people knew very well who was who. One Jewish lady was in shock when I found her and did not want to speak with me. She was closing the door and saying, "No, no, no."

'Then I prayed, "Lord, would you see that we have a good journey back?" Many gold mines are in this area that were once worked by prisoners. We came to a working mine, and the manager said, "I need to go back to Magadan in my helicopter. I will give you a ride." And in two hours I was back in Magadan.'

It's not an easy thing to help Jewish people in these remote areas. Just to get a photograph of them, to get their documents checked, or to get a passport can be an overwhelming task. It is a long-term process. In some cases we must send them to other republics to research their family history and obtain proof of their Jewishness.

In our first two years of fishing in eastern Siberia we saw over 2,000 *olim* leave for Israel. We brought them by air, bus or train – often hazardous and difficult journeys – to a small hotel in Khabarovsk to wait for Jewish Agency flights. I'll always remember one little lady on crutches I met there. She was about 4ft 6ins. The team said to me, 'Gustav, you must meet her, she is a special lady.' And then they whispered to me, 'She knows the Lord.'

They wanted to take a photo of us. She said, 'I am too small. Let's stand next to the staircase.' So she climbed up on the first step and said, 'I'm still too small.' She climbed up to the second step so she was on the same level with me. We photographed and had a glorious time. She was 81 years old and had practically no teeth, but her eyes were shining. She wanted to go home.

Our research has shown that there are thousands of Jewish people in the Far East, from Magadan right up to the Bering Strait. A vast territory! Many Jews came as prisoners and the survivors and their families continue to live there in exile. They often hide their Jewishness, making it impossible to know how many remain. But now they are revealing their Jewishness so that they may have a way of escape.

So often humanitarian aid is the key to get in these places and get a response. We've had 40–foot containers sent in from Western Europe and the United States. When we visit synagogues and tell the rabbis we want to share the vision of Operation Exodus only a small number of Jewish people turn up. But if we say we are bringing aid to their people we know that they will all turn up and it gives us opportunity to speak about going home.

One volunteer asked me, 'Would you like to visit the poorest of the poor?' I said, 'Yes,' though I don't find it easy to go into these homes to see utter misery. We drove there with our minibus and what moved my heart is that the children and the old ones came running out and embraced our volunteer. They had become friends and she said, 'Gustav, I have gained their confidence, now I am going to talk to them and tell them that it is time to go home.'

It is not easy to earn the trust of the Russian Jews. It takes time. It takes real commitment. I always say to our volunteers, 'Love never fails.' And so we break first into fallow ground, we water it and many times the Lord allows us to bring in the harvest.

From Siberia Elsa and I continued eastward by air to Alaska. It was a glorious day and I took in the snow-peaked mountains, glaciers, and valleys during the six-hour flight. It reminded me of a vision numerous believers have shared that one day large numbers of Jewish people would travel over this forsaken land, across the Bering Strait to Alaska.

Elsa was sitting behind me, also in a window seat, spying out the terrain from the air. The longer she looked the more she doubted that such a land route could be possible. 'There would be elderly people, children, invalids,' she thought. 'Wild animals inhabit the region such as Siberian tigers, bears, and wolves.' 'Lord,' she said in her spirit, 'if this is of you please give me a sign.'

As she continued to look out she saw a picture formed by the mountains, valleys, and crevices below. It was a large eagle with outstretched wings. Suddenly she remembered God's word to Moses in Exodus 19:4:

> *'You have seen what I did to the Egyptians, and how I bore you*
> *on eagles' wings and brought you to Myself.'*

I had the joy of speaking in a church in Alaska and sharing the possibility of an exodus across the Bering Strait. It was another of those electric meetings. The pastor came forward and said, 'We as a church have already made preparations to welcome the Jews when they come.'

Could circumstances really require such an escape route? I learned one lesson on our first trans-Siberian train journey that I've never forgotten. It happened on the border of Mongolia. The train came to a stop in a city called Chita. I asked Elsa to buy some bread while I wanted to take a few photographs. I had two small cameras, one for prints and one for slides. As I was taking these pictures I saw that my wife couldn't get anywhere near this wooden stall. Everybody was pushing. We were not in Britain there! And so I came and used my elbows, I admit, more effectively. I got to the front and put my cameras down to pay for the bread when I realized our train was slowly moving out of the station. In this part of the country a passenger train leaves only every three days. Elsa and I started running. We caught up to a rear compartment of the train, climbed on, and made our way forward to our own car. I settled down holding the two loaves of bread. 'Oh, **no**!' I cried. 'I've left the cameras behind.'

I was furious with myself. Both cameras gone! So I went to find an Intourist guide on the train and asked whether there was a lost and found office to report it. She laughed. 'Something like that doesn't exist in Russia.'

As I was still brooding over my loss the Lord spoke to me and said, 'So it will be with the Jews who are not going now. They will run for their lives and leave everything behind.'

Kjell Sjoberg once told me that he was praying aloud about our work as he walked in a Swedish forest. Suddenly a hunter appeared. 'Would you please be quiet!' he demanded. 'You're disturbing the animals.' Kjell saw it as a prophetic sign.

Anti-Semitism is not over. A young Jewish man we were helping to make *aliyah* in far-eastern Siberia was murdered six days before he was due to fly to Tel Aviv. A month previously the couple heading the Jewish Agency office in another Siberian city were badly beaten and robbed by men who told them, 'You have paid for your guilt to Russia – now you can go to Israel.' Our team helped them leave six days later.

Ultra-nationalist groups are openly inciting against the Jews in Siberia. I have seen signs on walls in cities; I have seen newspapers where they call for the extinction of the Jews. I have a strong sense we are in a countdown. This is born out by many of our intercessors, who have picked up in the Spirit that we are heading for turbulent times. The Lord has imprinted on us Zechariah 2:6:

> *'Up, up! Flee from the land of the north!'*

One night in our Bournemouth office the clock fell from the wall, smashed to the floor, and stopped working, the hands pointing at less than two minutes before midnight. We kept it as a reminder.

Sometimes we have tried to convey this to the Jews. Many were not ready to accept it. It's a human trait to hope that things will get better. Many told us, 'I will be the last one to go.' When Elsa told our Jewish partners in Odessa that the empty cabins on the 1993 sailings could mean Jewish lives one day, they thought she was over the top. Zionist activist Vladimir Jabotinsky received the same response when he attempted to warn European Jews in the 1930s.

Not only in Alaska, but as I have travelled throughout North America and Europe I have come across churches, fellowships and individual believers who are making preparations to help the Jewish people on their way home. A friend shared a dream in which he saw how they were persecuted, how they could not even escape from one country to the next. He saw bloodshed and terrible scenes. There was only one safe destination – Israel.

When he woke he wept before the Lord and asked why there was no one to help His people. The Lord showed him a big world map with many little flashing lights and he realized these were the Bible-believing Christians who would help the Jewish people on their way home.

In our generation, as in the Holocaust, Christians may once again be challenged to lay down their lives for the kinsfolk of Messiah. '*Inasmuch as you did it to one of the least of these My brethren,*' the King will answer us one day, '*you did it to Me.*'

CHAPTER 9

A Divine Task

The Sovereign LORD declares—
he who gathers the exiles of Israel:
"I will gather still others to them
besides those already gathered."
Isaiah 56:8 (NIV)

Gustav Scheller lived to see Ebenezer complete 100 Operation Exodus sailings. Sadly, he wasn't aboard the *Dmitry Shostakovich* when the Ukrainian ship docked at Haifa on 8th December 1999. That historic trip brought 379 more Jewish people back to the land of their forefathers. However, Gustav did take part in the celebration at Jerusalem via telephone link-up later that day – from his hospital bed in England. Significantly, the gathering took place in the same hotel where Operation Exodus had been born in January 1991. So it's not surprising that Gustav was full of joy when he spoke.

'I'm so grateful to the Lord for the way He led us to expand the work of Ebenezer step by step,' he told leaders, volunteers, national co-ordinators and supporters. 'It's God's doing and I want to give Him all the honour and all the glory,' he added, reflecting on the ministry's tremendous growth. He was happy in his belief of how God had provided the right resources at the right time – especially personnel and finances. 'He's truly the best administrator,' said Gustav. It was the last time many of the listeners heard their leader. For he died just a few weeks later.

However, his legacy took root – and the ministry continued to expand through the vastness of the former Soviet Union (fSU). Ebenezer opened more offices across this vast territory and gained more help from fSU churches – backed by an increasing number of national co-ordinators around the world. In fulfilment of biblical prophecy, the Jewish people have returned to Israel literally from *'the ends of the earth'* – émigrés from Siberia and the Russian Far East being prime examples. 'Please don't underestimate the value of your work,' was the conclusion from the *Sochnut* (Jewish Agency) director for the region. 'Virtually no one goes home from this region without having been helped by Ebenezer.'

In the mid 1990s, our teams started to help the Jewish people return home from the five Muslim-dominated Central Asian republics – Kazakhstan, Uzbekistan, Kyrgyzstan, Turkmenistan and Tajikistan. Kazakhstan is by far the biggest country. 'Fishing' teams – who make the initial links – range far and wide from the main base in Almaty, often travelling 20 hours and more by train to find Jewish people and urge them to go home. Increasingly, the message is backed up by distribution of humanitarian aid – food, clothing, medicines and even special items such as hearing aids. Christian love in action has made a deep impact among God's ancient people.

Viktor Osadchi is a prime example. A widower in his fifties, Viktor was scraping an existence for himself and his three children by looking after deer in the harsh Chukotskiy region in the far north of Siberia when he was met by Sergey and Zhenya, a young couple serving as Ebenezer volunteers. They told him of the opportunity to make a new start in the land of his forefathers. And so hope dawned in Viktor's heart. His life had been one of dashed hopes and tragedy, culminating in his wife dying through vodka addiction. He and his children were surviving on dry bread when the volunteers found him. However, Ebenezer took care of all their needs – including apartment rental and new clothes – while the process to gain the necessary documents to make *aliyah* moved to completion. Today they are in the Promised Land.

Such work has grown – and many base leaders raised up – under the leadership of Troels and Birgit Truelsen from Sweden. They have faithfully served as operational leaders in the fSU for many years. Among those who've benefited from their guidance are Boris and Elya Vasyukov. They have played an important role in this part of the world, carrying the torch that has been passed on from Gustav. From humble beginnings in the small town of Neryungri, Yakutia, they had become involved in praying for new leaders of Ebenezer's operations at Khabarovsk, one of Russia's main administrative centres, not far from the Chinese border. 'We were so unwilling to leave our ministry in the church,' Boris recalled, 'since we were fully committed to the building up of a new congregation. However, while praying for new Ebenezer leaders in Khabarovsk, I received a very clear call from the Lord.' So in June 1997 they became a part of Operation Exodus – by heading Ebenezer's office in the Far East of Russia.

Their dedicated colleagues have promoted *aliyah* among the Jewish communities of Armenia, a country especially dear to Gustav's heart, and in neighbouring Georgia. Operation Exodus started there, in Joseph Stalin's homeland, in 1998. There are many more Jewish people living there than in Armenia – and the work has been making a deep impact among them. Training local Christians to 'fish' for Jews has been a priority. With strong prayer backing in the churches, teams regularly collect *olim* and transport them by minibus to Tbilisi for Jewish Agency flights to Tel Aviv. In Georgia, as in other parts of the fSU, the teams' love is expressed practically through aid distribution to the poor and needy. Their compassion has broken through the barricades between Christians and Jews.

Our work across this continent entered a significant phase in 1999. For Operation Exodus started in Moldova and Belarus.

Jewish people had suffered horrendously during the Holocaust in these two countries in the western part of the fSU – along with those in Ukraine. In Belarus, considered to have a highly anti-Semitic, totalitarian government, Operation Exodus helped around 1,300 Jewish people reach the Promised Land within the first six months of setting up base in Minsk. Operation Exodus started working in Moldova three months later. Hundreds of Jews were taken by bus to join the ship in Odessa – or have since reached Israel by Jewish Agency flights.

To develop this – along with the rest of the work – Boris and Elya were invited to head Ebenezer's office in Moscow in 2000. Soon, Jewish people living in this historic city were being helped to make *aliyah* – and Operation Exodus teams were breaking new ground in the Russian Federation. One of the areas where Moscow team members started working was Dagestan, the mountainous Caucasian republic on the Caspian Sea. Today the Moscow base has oversight of 18 *oblasts*, or provinces, of central Russia. During 2000 Ebenezer also set up an intensive training programme in the eastern Ukraine for local Christians to help spread the vision of making *aliyah* among the 40,000 Jewish people living in the Donetsk Oblast (a governmental region), the country's mining heartland.

Changes loomed again four years later. Around this time, the leadership sought God's guidance about the sailings. They felt the days of fishing in these lands could be limited, and a time of persecution could be getting closer. A team of intercessors was asked to spend a few days waiting for God's direction. During this time, they felt drawn to a scripture from 2 Samuel 5:22-25. This happened three times through independent prayer partners. The context of the story is King David seeking God for battle strategies against the Philistines. When he asks God the first time, '*Shall I go up*' (vs 19-20), the answer comes, '*Go up*', followed by an act of deliverance. The Philistines gather to strike again. But when David asks God for a plan this time round, the response is different:

> *Therefore David inquired of the Lord, and He said, "You shall not go up; circle around behind them, and come upon them in front of the mulberry trees. And it shall be, when you hear the sound of marching in the tops of the mulberry trees, then you shall advance quickly. For then the Lord will go out before you..." (vs 23,24)*

The team felt there was a lesson from these verses. The ministry had entered a new season – and Ebenezer should be open to new ways and strategies. The leadership felt they should not plan sailings for the immediate future. So at their meeting in September 2004, the EEFI Board decided the sailing programme would be suspended. This also seemed to send a powerful signal of prophetic significance to a number of Jewish people in the fSU. A serious season was coming, and safe exit routes may not always be open to them. Financial issues were not even considered.

Ebenezer began a church development ministry in 2007. That involved equipping and preparing local congregations in the fSU for *aliyah*. Though a mountain of challenges has emerged over the years, our teams in the fSU have not only faced them – but also covered much ground for God's people. They have overseen the formation of the prayer network across central Russia, which took nine years to achieve. But the hard work was worth it. For now they have more than 2,500 prayer partners. They have also seen through the setting up of a financial partners network across that region.

Churches in the fSU have been very fortunate. For many years, Christians there not only heard talks about the exodus of the Jewish people, but also could actually see *aliyah* starting to happen. Many have taken part in helping Jewish people make *aliyah*. 'I believe God has blessed our churches in a special way,' said Boris, 'so they could assume responsibility and take the burden of caring for Jewish people in the near future.' In fact, he feels Ebenezer's 18-year experience in the fSU countries is invaluable for the development of its wider work.

The commitment shown by our workers is remarkable. Ebenezer's teams in the east continue to help and support more than 70 per cent of all those making *aliyah* from the regions where we operate. In the Central Asian countries of Kazakhstan, Turkmenistan, Kyrgyzstan and Tajikistan the figure is 100 per cent. 'This is truly a wonderful tribute and testimony to the faithfulness of our dedicated workers throughout this vast area spanning ten countries,' said International Co-ordinator Alan Field. 'We're also moving forward with our strategy to strengthen and hand over greater responsibility to our national teams in these countries.'

Inspired by a passage from the first book of Kings which referred to '*the young leaders of the provinces*', Ebenezer plans to release an emerging generation of leaders to take on the challenge in these countries. 'An effective vision will always empower, release and prepare people for the future, while also having its roots in the past,' said Alan. 'That's what we're working to achieve.' In 2009 Ebenezer Operation Exodus was able to help more than 3,000 Jewish people make *aliyah* from our base operations in the East. Our teams visited almost 13,000 Jewish families to bring comfort and the message of *aliyah*. They also helped more than 1,000 Jewish families visit consular officials and assisted nearly 400 to apply for their documents and papers. Teams have distributed more than 2,500 much needed food parcels and provided medicines for Holocaust survivors.

One rabbi's story offers an interesting endorsement for Ebenezer's work in the east. He really wasn't interested in meeting an Operation Exodus team. He wanted nothing to do with Christians. But on the road from Tbilisi to Batumi, along Georgia's south-western border with Turkey, the team phoned him again. This time the answer was different – yes, they could come to his home for ten minutes. He was waiting for them with his wife and children. No sooner had they sat down than the questions began.

'I've heard about your work,' said the rabbi, 'why are you Christians helping Jews?' The team leader told him it's written in the Hebrew Bible, the *Tanakh,* that a massive exodus, far greater than the one from Egypt, would take place – and non-Jews would help in this. Today God, not Ebenezer, was gathering His people, he told the man. The questions continued to come thick and fast. The rabbi softened. 'You and your workers are welcome in our home any time,' he said. 'You really have a divine task.'

CHAPTER 10

The Global Jewish Family

> *Therefore behold, the days are coming," says the Lord, "that it shall no more be said, 'The Lord lives who brought up the children of Israel from the land of Egypt,' but, 'The Lord lives who brought up the children of Israel from the land of the north and from all the lands where He had driven them.'*
>
> Jeremiah 16:14,15

It's a modern expression of ancient prophecy. Old Testament seers spoke of God's people returning not only from the land of the north – but also from all the nations. Strangely enough, Ebenezer's international work has grown to such an extent that Operation Exodus currently has representatives in more than 40 countries.

A simple coupon from a local Christian bookshop helped provide an answer to her lifelong search. For since she was a little girl, Debra Minotti had wanted to know the history of the Jewish people. She went to the store in question and came across Operation Exodus. There was just one copy left, so she traded her coupon for that. She read it in 24 hours and contacted the Ebenezer office in Bournemouth straightaway.

That was in 2000. And it was the start of a new journey for Debra. Eventually she served as a volunteer in the Ukraine for six months, and then helped develop the ministry in the UK.

'Working with the Bournemouth team has been a highlight,' she recalled. 'I learned so much from watching them.' The biggest step was yet to come. In 2004 she became National Co-ordinator for the USA.

According to 2007 figures, there are 6.4 million Jews in the States. That's a million more than in Israel. Those Jews make up more than two per cent of America's population. With more than one-and-a-half million, New York has the largest Jewish population of any state. California has over a million, Florida has just over a half and New Jersey just under a half. More than 60 per cent of America's Jews live in these four states. If any nation was a key target for Ebenezer's attention, this must be one.

Debra returned home and began a new work for Ebenezer USA. Originally established in North Carolina several years previously, this new home for the American ministry was based in a small office at her church, in Buffalo, New York state. They were humble beginnings. She had no computer and no prayer team. Realising it was important to take one step at a time, she tried to follow the maxim, 'do small things with great love'. Said Debra, 'It's a powerful thing. I don't think people understand the power of the small. I knew if we did these small things well, God would take care of the big things…and people started coming along, helping out'.

An astonishing process started as the work grew in 'miraculous little ways' – as Debra describes them. 'My sister went to the bank,' she recalled, 'and all of a sudden there was a Jewish man who started talking to her. They spoke about *aliyah*. He was from Russia. He wasn't even from America.' Debra's own church was a great support. Helpers would come and go, and the fledgling team would look at where the large Jewish populations were. 'It kind of started growing, and the Lord would take us to the next phase.'

Their first major breakthrough came in 2006. Yael called the Buffalo office. She was a young Orthodox Jew who wanted to make *aliyah*. She'd seen our website and wanted some assistance. Then Yael mentioned she hadn't informed the Jewish Agency she was contacting a Christian organisation. Debra was concerned about this, and wanted to make sure Ebenezer's work was totally transparent. 'We really prayed,' she said, 'and I realised I had to talk to the Jewish Agency.' A relationship started between Ebenezer and the Jewish Agency in the States, a group of churches offered a gift of 500 dollars, and Yael finally made her homecoming in 2007. It was a sign that the American team had to prepare to help others who might want to make *aliyah*, too. So they prayed even more.

They decided the ideal would be a 'hub' – a facility not only to support those making *aliyah* but also to help churches in their ministry to the Jewish people. The Ebenezer team undertook a number of prayer walks, including one in New York City. 'We were in New York and we asked the Lord for a hub. Within a few weeks, a man called and said, "We have some space in Connecticut (just outside New York) – would you like to have a look at it?" At the same time, a physiotherapist was purchasing a building in Alaska. A couple of months later he said to our representative there, "I think I need to give you some space".' It was a remarkable series of events. Eventually, Ebenezer had not only their existing office in Buffalo – but also two new hubs in Connecticut and Alaska.

Another major step forward has been the increase of committed intercessors from only a handful to almost 900 in five years. They also have more than 300 churches of various denominations on their database. So far, they have assisted 33 Jews to return to Israel. 'We just help those who want to make *aliyah* and we pray.' It's not always smooth. 'God brings such encouragement when at times you're discouraged,' Debra admitted, 'often it's when and where you least expect it.' She confessed it's quite a challenge being National Co-ordinator in a country with close to six million Jewish people: 'There are many open doors – but the workers are few'.

There have been similar developments further south, in Latin America. 'We're experiencing extraordinary open doors like never before in Mexico and other Latin American countries,' said Regional Co-ordinator Heriberto Gonzalez. The list of invitations received to promote Ebenezer's vision early in 2010 was bigger than all previous invitations combined since 1991, when the ministry started in Mexico. 'The work is growing at an increasing rate,' added Heriberto.

Meetings at different churches and among ministerial alliances in several states of Mexico were held in 2009. They reached more than 5,000 believers – 'with extraordinary results'. Hundreds of intercessors have joined the work, and the team cannot make all the proposed visits and meetings, such is the demand. 'It's amazing to see even among Mexican indigenous people – who make their living off the land with very little wealth – the message has been received with joy,' said Heriberto. 'Considering their economic situation, their financial contributions to bless Israel have been much greater than those received in our modern cities.'

The work in Latin America was pioneered by pastor Roger Wolcott in 1987. He visited churches with the rallying call from the book of Psalms to *'pray for the peace of Jerusalem'*. Enrique Porras remembers those early days and how they affected him. 'When the invitation was given to pray for Ebenezer ministry, I volunteered to participate by praying daily in my church,' he recalled. Based in Monterrey, Mexico, Enrique translated prayer letters, distributed bi-monthly journals and assisted at events. He took part in the Jerusalem Prayer Conference in 1991 and went on to help the Ebenezer board in Mexico. Now he's part of the core team with Roger and Heriberto. But when asked about the part he plays, he responds with humility. 'My role in the Ebenezer ministry is to pray,' he said, 'wait on the Lord and collaborate in the prayer network helping develop what the Holy Spirit guides us to do as a body.'

Often there are surprises. In 2004, a team from Ebenezer

visited Colombia and discovered intercession was already underway for Israel. In the capital Bogotá, International Development Director Theo Abbenhuis saw a discouraging sign – some anti-Semitic graffiti. Yet the following year, he visited Maranatha Church in Vitoria do Santa Fe – which has a ministry involving more than 4,000 congregations wanting to know God's direction in relation to Israel.

Heriberto outlined a new challenge for Ebenezer in Latin America – the *Sephardic Jews*. 'They've just begun to surface after 500 years of obscurity,' he said, 'remnants of the Spanish and the New World (American continent) Inquisitions. They've suddenly discovered the only way to be healed and to fulfil their God-given destiny is to gain a clear understanding of their historical roots and by making *aliyah*.' Heriberto linked them to a quote from the Old Testament book of Obadiah which refers to exiles from Jerusalem who are *'in Sepharad'* (Obadiah v 20). What he calls 'divine contacts' have been made in cities where historically, Jewish exiles eventually settled during the Inquisition period. These contacts include pastors from Bogotá and La Havana in Cuba.

'The discovery of the Americas by Christopher Columbus occurred when Jewish people were forced to either convert or leave Spain,' Heriberto explained, outlining some of the historical background. 'Many joined Columbus' fleet. One was his translator, Luis de Torres, believed to be the first Jewish descendant in Cuba. After the Spanish-American War, more Jews immigrated to the island. The next migration of Jews to Cuba occurred in the years following World War I, when many Jewish people suffered through anti-Semitism and increasing Nazi persecution.'

The message has been spreading across the continent. Ebenezer Mexico held three successful conferences in 2006-7, sharing their conviction about the homecoming of the Jews with more than 2,000 people from various churches. In January 2007 Roger held a lunch meeting at Mexico City where people from a wide range of evangelical churches expressed their commitment to the Jewish people with Israeli Ambassador Yosef Livne. In turn, the ambassador shared his hope of Israel being a nation where 'the children of Ishmael, the children of Bethlehem and the Jews, can live peacefully in harmony'. Described by the Latin American team as 'historic', the event culminated in people praying for the ambassador – while he prayed for God's blessings over Mexico.

In spring 2009, a team from Switzerland prepared for a special journey through Argentina to pray for Latin American Jews. Representing three Christian organisations – including Ebenezer – they studied some history about the region before the trip, and uncovered some wrongdoings by their forefathers. 'We discovered the Swiss Red Cross had helped many Nazis to flee to South America,' said Switzerland Prayer Co-ordinator Hanna Ernst, 'especially Argentina, where the largest number of Jewish immigrants in the region live. Today many Holocaust survivors, and their descendants, live side by side with their former persecutors.'

When they embarked on their expedition, the team stayed at a Bible school in the capital Buenos Aires. They found out some of the buildings had been used seventy years ago by the Nazis as an espionage centre. 'We saw how the God of Israel can turn a curse into blessing,' said Hanna, who is also wife of Ebenezer's Chairman Markus Ernst. 'In the school we found much potential for helping to fulfil the Lord's purposes for Israel – 400 students preparing for ministry in the Spanish-speaking world. During our week in Buenos Aires, God led us through important prayer times at various sites, as well as precious encounters with Jewish people and organisations.'

A seismic change has been felt across the ocean in Africa, too. 'It's clear the emphasis of *aliyah* has expanded from the former Soviet Union to the western countries,' said National Co-ordinator for South Africa Alida Schoultz, 'And for that matter it includes the south. America, UK, Canada, France,

South Africa and some other countries are suddenly sending hundreds of *olim* to Israel.' Millions still remain in these countries, but Alida is convinced these hundreds of *olim* are just 'a wake-up call' to prepare for a mass *aliyah*. 'When we decided to partner with the Jewish Agency in South Africa – and then also in the UK by sponsoring flights – I'm sure this was just the beginning,' she explained.

It was in 1995 that Alida first went to Odessa to serve as a volunteer with Ebenezer for three months. She went back in 1996, this time serving for nine months. On the last sailing for the year in December, Gustav asked her to become National Co-ordinator for South Africa. So what did that mean? 'As National Co-ordinator of a country, you're especially responsible to share God's Word regarding the return of the Jewish people in churches and other groups,' she explained. 'Over the years I've met with hundreds – maybe even thousands – of people who were so surprised to hear this message, and even more surprised to learn it's being fulfilled in our time.'

Initially, it appeared *aliyah* was not high on the agenda for South African Jews. Those who left mainly went to Australia and a few other countries. 'We often prayed God would work in the hearts of the South African Jews to make *aliyah* instead,' said Alida, 'but at the same time often wondered what God will have to do to convince them.' In 2008 things changed. Hundreds of Jews visited the Jewish Agency office to apply for *aliyah*. Special flights were arranged and within twelve months, four flights with a total of 400 *olim* made *aliyah*.

Ebenezer Operation Exodus decided to partner with the Jewish Agency by sponsoring the flights. As National Co-ordinator, Alida contacted them and became involved in a way she never expected. 'I was asked to address the *olim* the day before they left,' she recalled. 'As I stood before those precious people – with a well-prepared speech – I was overcome by tears. I recalled the many times I'd addressed Russian *olim*.

Never in my wildest dreams did I think I'd have the opportunity to address *olim* from my home country. I consider it as one of the highlights of my time with Ebenezer.'

Alida was invited to join one of the flights to Israel in 2009. 'This was by far the greatest honour and privilege I've experienced,' she remembered. 'Again, I was reminded of my first days in Odessa and the overwhelming emotions when I met the first group of *olim* at the railway station, accompanying them by bus to the port, and being on my first sailing with them to Israel. But nothing could prepare me for the honour and privilege to accompany a group of eighty-five *olim* by plane from South Africa.' She spent the first two days of the absorption process with them in Jerusalem, and joined them for their welcome ceremony at the Western Wall. 'To experience God's Word fulfilled in our days and be right in the midst of it touches your heart.'

People across the African continent have been helped by Ebenezer. In 2006 an aid fund project was underway to feed Jewish schoolchildren in Ethiopia. In co-operation with Jewish funding organisation *Keren Heyesod*, the scheme initially supported one meal a day for the 2,400 who attended a school in Gondar, as part of the preparations for the remaining *Falash Mura* people to leave for Israel. The *Falash Mura* had been virtually unknown until the airlifting programme *Operation Solomon* in 1991. Ebenezer helped carry the baton in 2008, by co-sponsoring a homecoming flight for more than 100 Ethiopian Jewish immigrants. It was a poignant part of the journey when they passed over the length of the Red Sea, scene of the first exodus in Old Testament times. 'There was a holy atmosphere and expectancy,' recalled Switzerland Administrator Urs Kasermann, who was part of the Ebenezer team on the flight. 'Finally, our Ethiopian friends had reached the end of their exile.' He watched émigrés step onto the tarmac when their plane landed at Ben Gurion airport, Tel Aviv. 'When they felt it under their feet, some of them fell on their knees and kissed the ground.'

In summer 2009, Urs was invited to speak at the All Africa Pastors' Conference in Lagos, Nigeria. 'It was a climax when I was allowed to lead 500-700 pastors from all Africa in prayer for Israel during a 24-hour prayer watch for one hour,' he said. 'Many of the pastors came up to me afterwards, saying, "We were told to pray for Israel, and so we did – but we didn't know why. Now, after your teaching, we have understood and in future we'll stand in the gap for Israel".' In addition, they wanted to help by supporting *aliyah* financially. 'It's amazing to see how God calls people to deep intercession,' said Urs, 'especially in Africa.'

But Africa is almost on Israel's doorstep, compared to other countries. The nation farthest away from the Promised Land is New Zealand. Yet people there have supported *aliyah* with prayer, finance and voluntary work since 1991. The team sense a new thing is happening, and are actively praying for the return of more than 6,000 New Zealand Jews. 'Although happily settled, the time will come when they'll return,' said National Co-ordinator Anne Higgins.

She became involved after meeting Gustav Scheller and Steve Lightle at the International Prayer Conference at Jerusalem in 1988. People had gathered to pray from nearly 30 nations, for the peace of that city. 'The immersion in fellowship, all-night prayer and intense teaching opened my eyes to the divine purposes of God for Israel,' explained Anne. Three years later, Gustav was drawing her deeper into the work – and the result was the emergence of Ebenezer New Zealand.

Spring 2008 saw an Operation Exodus tour of churches there – with Steve Lightle as the main speaker, supported by a six-strong team from Ebenezer. People filled the churches with expectation to hear Steve's message. One pastor wished he could have spoken on four days and nights – instead of just one night. A Bible college reportedly described Steve's teaching as 'quite revealing', and had received many requests for the recording of his talks. 'A new phase in the work is beginning,' said Anne.

Not far from her is Australia – home to 120,000 Jews. Across this vast but sparsely populated continent, Operation Exodus prayer leaders and groups are praying for the '*aliyah* highways' to be opened for God's people when they are called home. Philippa Kirk originally served as an Operation Exodus volunteer on a 'fishing' team in Far East Russia. Now back home in Victoria, Philippa is Australian Prayer Co-ordinator.

During preparations for the 2009 UK-Australia Prayer Initiative, Operation Exodus prayer leaders in England passed on some research. One of the significant events they had discovered was the deportation of Jewish men of German and Austrian descent from Britain to Australia during World War II. Regarded as a threat to national security, these men had been classed as enemy aliens. On 10th September 1940, *HMT Dunera* had departed from Liverpool, England, carrying 2,524 'enemy aliens' – of whom more than 2,000 were Jewish refugees escaping Nazi rule in Austria and Germany. The deportees were treated as prisoners and experienced severe deprivation and maltreatment during the voyage. On arrival in Sydney, they were sent to internment camps in the rural towns of Hay, New South Wales, and Tatura in northern Victoria.

Equipped with this background knowledge, Philippa led prayer teams onto both of these former internment campsites. 'We stood on the site of the camp in Hay,' she said, 'and declared the word of God from Jeremiah 29:10-14':

> *For thus says the Lord: After seventy years are completed…I will visit you and perform My good word toward you…I will bring you back from your captivity, I will gather you from all the nations and from the places where I have driven you.*

Philippa and her team sensed the time had come for Jews to be regathered from Australia and allowed to return home to Israel. The following April, Sydney Prayer Co-ordinator Christine Cuming came back from a Jewish community function, at which the President of the NSW Zionist Federation had announced. 'There has been a dramatic increase in *aliyah* from Australia in the first months of this year [2010]'.

From the Operation Exodus base in Sydney, activities are co-ordinated for the family of nations across South East Asia–Oceania. 'It was a phone call one evening ten years ago that started it all for us,' said Pete Stucken, who holds responsibility for this task, and whose wife Fiona serves as Prayer Co-ordinator for the region. The couple are from a business background and joined Operation Exodus in 2002. They felt prompted to make contact with Noel and Barbara Bell, founders of Intercessors for Australia which had become the foundation for a national prayer movement. Gustav had met both of them in 1986 at a prophetic gathering of leaders on Mount Carmel. Gustav had later asked Noel to oversee the work of Operation Exodus in Australia.

'Noel imparted to us his heart for *aliyah*,' Pete recalled. 'Then during our first visit to Israel [in 2002], a transaction took place in our hearts. The Lord showed us bringing the Jews back to Israel was a priority for Him, and He was giving us opportunity to become involved. Five years on, and our office has become the base for Operation Exodus SE Asia Oceania. Work stops when the daily mail arrives. Perhaps we'll open a gnarled and battered envelope that's been posted somewhere in the highlands of Papua New Guinea. The handwritten note inside might simply say: "We're praying for the *aliyah*". At other times an envelope from Papua New Guinea will bear a bank note carefully wrapped in sheets of paper, just with the words "for *aliyah*". With tender, thankful hearts, we pause to pray multiplied blessing on our Papua New Guinea intercessors. Their partnership is vital in preparing the *aliyah* highways for the Jews of Oceania and south-east Asia. Operation Exodus is truly an intercessory ministry.'

Understanding that Ebenezer Operation Exodus is entering

a new season of intercession involving co-operation across international boundaries, Pete and Fiona have looked towards building up prayer teams in neighbouring nations. In April 2010 they gathered a prayer team in Singapore. 'We see Singapore as a key gateway and transit point in south-east Asia,' said Fiona. 'Israel Defence Forces officers helped train Singapore's fledgling defence force in the 1960s. This has fostered a deep-seated sense of gratitude to Israel for her help in time of need. There are small communities of Jews in Singapore as well as other Asian nations, and we see Singapore as having a calling to facilitate and assist the *aliyah* from Oceania.' Nine local prayer partners including a church elder joined them as they climbed up to Fort Canning Park, representing a gateway to the city, a seat of government prior to and during World War II. 'We prayed and proclaimed Scripture together, that *aliyah* highways would be open through Singapore.'

A delightful surprise awaited Pete and Fiona when they visited Malaysia in March 2010. In a nation with a vocal and at times intimidating Moslem majority, they discovered an openness to Israel and a willingness to pray for *aliyah* among Christians who'd gathered for a Passover banquet and conference. They feel God is 'on the move' in Asia, engaging believers with a desire to participate in His plan to restore His people to their land.

A similar awakening is also happening as far away as China. Even descendants of the *Kaifeng* Jews in China are returning to Israel. A recent report in the *New York Times* (4th April 2010) uncovered this forgotten community – said to number about fifty – who are allegedly embracing their legacy and returning to Jewish ways. Their forefathers were *Sephardic Jew* traders and refugees who came along the Silk Road to Kaifeng, capital of the Northern Song Dynasty from the tenth to twelfth century. Those ancestors even built a synagogue – since replaced by a hospital – and one of their scrolls is now kept at the British Museum in London. Over the years, a number of books have been written about the Chinese Jews. Among the most recent has been *The Jews Of Kaifeng, China* by Xu Xin (KTAV Publishing House, 2003). 'Many reports confirm the impression that the surviving Kaifeng Jewish descendants still have a special feeling for their roots,' said the author, 'as evidenced by their openness in confirming that they are descended from Jews, their desire to learn more about Jewish history and culture, and their willingness to contact Jews who live outside of China.'

Ebenezer is hearing more and more about such so-called 'lost tribes'. Allegedly they also include the ancient *Bnei Menashe* tribe of India, who claim their ancestry goes back as far as Manasseh, one of Joseph's sons. An Ebenezer team learned about them during a trip to Mumbai in December 2008. 'A lady who works among Jewish drug addicts in India made an appointment for us to meet the director of ORT, a Jewish vocational training institute,' said National Co-ordinator Deepa Thomas. 'He said he could only meet us for 30 minutes at the most, but then he got a phone call postponing his main appointment until the next day. This convinced him our meeting was God's plan and he extended it to two hours! This has resulted in numerous openings and possibilities for *aliyah* from India.

'We learned at this meeting there is a large community of poor *Bnei Menashe* labourers in Manipur who've been marginalised and ignored. ORT offered to give a number of them vocational training before making *aliyah*. Before that can be done, however, we need to go to the community and convince them of their need to make *aliyah*. ORT also opened the way to meet and help poor Jewish people from another tribe, the *Bnei Ephraim*, in Andhra Pradesh state.' The BBC news website carried a story about the *Bnei Menashe* group in 2005, reporting that one of Israel's chief rabbis recognised the 6,000-strong community as lost descendants of ancient Jews. It was a controversial judgement, but *Bnei Menashe* members welcomed it, delighted they could now 'go to the Promised Land'.

Theo and Els Abbenhuis had joined Ebenezer in 1998, after living and working in Israel for another organisation. They returned to Jerusalem in 2004 to support Operation Exodus activities in the nations. 'We speak at international conferences and Jewish events and to the media,' said Theo, 'providing information and understanding about what God is doing as he re-gathers the Jewish people from all countries. It's our belief we're on the threshold of a massive *aliyah* – and need to be ready to assist ever-greater numbers of *olim*, as we witness continually rising violence and public demonstrations against Jews everywhere, along with economic shakings. So we're sounding the *shofar*, so to speak, challenging believers everywhere to help the Jews in their return to Israel while they still have the freedom and opportunity.'

Urs Kasermann works 'in full harmony' with the international team, as he puts it. For although he is National Co-ordinator for Switzerland, that means he's also in charge of developing the French-speaking countries – France, Belgium, French-speaking Africa – as well as Nigeria, Ghana, Austria and Italy. 'I have the privilege to build up teams in these countries, and to co-operate with them to develop Ebenezer's work in these nations,' he said. 'It's always a great pleasure to work with all the international team.'

He used to be a businessman, but saw his company fail in 2000. He lost all his money and property. Following this major crisis, Urs and wife Caroline attended an Ebenezer prayer seminar at Berne in 2004. There, he met International Chairman Markus Ernst – who mentioned the organisation was looking for a National Co-ordinator for Switzerland. Eventually, Urs applied for the post and the board appointed him. He started in 2005. 'I'm so grateful to the Lord for calling me to this job,' he said. 'Indeed, I don't consider it a mere job – but a calling of God to stand with the Jewish people.'

Now Urs is seeing that same call go out to other people to lead teams in other countries. 'In some countries we had to pray for three years before God showed us the right person,' he said. 'We see how God opens the doors to Jewish organisations such as the Jewish Agency – as well as to individual Jews.' A particular prayer concern had been for teams and National Co-ordinators in France, Austria and Belgium. 'During the last couple of years, we could see God's goodness,' he admitted, 'and today we can count on a team in France and Austria and a National Co-ordinator in Belgium.'

His team has developed contacts with Jewish groups. Through those connections, they helped the first Jewish family from France to make *aliyah* in 2007, and the first family from Switzerland with their homecoming in 2008. That process continued with another young family from Switzerland in October 2009. 'God has also led Caroline and me to accompany this family on their flight to Israel,' Urs explained. 'Not knowing each other's schedule, we had booked the same flight. Even more, the family was booked by the Jewish Agency – and we were seated right behind them! So we were able to accompany them to Tel Aviv.'

It's all very well hearing about the homecoming journeys, but how do they work at the destination point? What happens to people once they arrive? Overseeing that section of the work is Olim Liaison Shirley Lawrenson. Now based in Jerusalem, she has been part of more than 120 sailings. 'It's been amazing to see how God went before us,' she explained, 'and allowed every sailing with the *olim* onboard to arrive home safely to Eretz Israel. Despite many challenges during the sailings, we could always trust that the Lord answered our prayers – and the prayers of many intercessors around the world. During the sailing we've seen how God brought storms to a calm, healed people, protected the ship in difficult circumstances and touched people's hearts.'

Shirley has also been involved in visiting *olim* as they return home, bringing comfort and support when they are in need. 'Since the opening of the Ebenezer office in Jerusalem in 2006, I've been involved in bringing practical help to needy *olim* at their homes. During the 2006 Lebanon war we were able to reach out to Jewish people in the north of Israel as they faced the conflict. Since then we've continued to encourage *aliyah* from different nations and assist *olim* as they take their first steps in the land.' Their needs include finding jobs and learning the language, so Ebenezer helps by locating other organisations that can serve them in those specific areas. We have also assisted in other practical ways by providing help with food parcels, school utilities and payments for medicine. 'It's also become clear many *olim* just need a place where they can visit and relate to someone who cares. They need a friend, a listening ear, some advice – and encouragement that the big step to make *aliyah* was the right step.' Shirley's team has seen *aliyah* flights from all over the world.

Jeff Holloway leads the work in the UK. But he first became involved with Ebenezer as an intercessor in 2001. Four years later, he was challenged at a conference about organising a prayer meeting in his hometown. 'I was the only one there from Rochdale,' Jeff recalled, 'so we started a prayer group, which developed into my being appointed county rep for North Manchester and South East Lancashire.' He has since become the UK National Director. 'In my local area we've begun to form relationships and links with the Manchester Jewish community,' he explained. 'Before this we'd attended various events to get ourselves known.'

Ebenezer is certainly becoming known. UK trustee Beverley Hill recalled one 'special day' for the Bournemouth office when Rafi Nassi, the Jewish Agency's newly appointed UK Director for Aliyah, came to visit. This was the first time in the 18-year history of the ministry that anyone from the JA had come to the head office in the basement of Ebenezer House in England. Rafi had come in May 2009 to seek a partnership with the first official JA *aliyah* flight from the UK. The trustees responded positively to this opportunity which had been covered in prayer over many years for the right timing.

The focus was to be on families and the younger generation. It was to be called the 'Red Carpet' programme. Thanks to the generous giving of UK supporters, Ebenezer provided financial aid that covered a series of lectures on making *aliyah*, Hebrew language classes, pre-flight transport and accommodation costs in the UK and arrival costs in Israel. Members of the UK team attended some of lectures and language classes and were privileged to accompany the *olim* on their homecoming.

The first flight to Israel took place on 11th August 2009, taking 107 Jewish immigrants from London to Tel Aviv. During the five-hour journey the team answered many questions about Ebenezer's involvement. First people to board the El Al flight were three-month-old baby boy Naphtali and 90-year-old Lina. Dov, his wife and eight children, had intended to move to Israel at a later date – but were so impressed by the organisation and excitement generated for this special flight, they decided to join. In Israel, Dov will continue to work for his present employer as a computer programmer via the internet. Leal was a 21-year-old woman travelling alone, but joining relatives in Eilat. She was keen to learn Hebrew thoroughly in her desire to work with children. Daniel, the son of a market trader, had left Leeds and hopes to join the Israel Defence Force. Simon, 40, was being reunited with his brother who is a rabbi in Israel and will live on a kibbutz and study hotel management. He was full of thanks for Ebenezer's help in enabling him to make *aliyah*.

On board, Jeff Holloway entertained the children by making balloon animals. `Especially poignant comments came from 18 and 19-year-olds who knew they would be called into the Israel Defence Force,' said Jeff. Grateful parents chatted to Ebenezer's Area Representative Rod Langston, who explained why the team were helping them make *aliyah*. UK Chairman of

Trustees Ken Hepworth discovered he was sitting next to a journalist from Israel News Channel 1, resulting in an interview for a Jewish Agency film on UK *aliyah*. Regular El Al passengers showed much interest in Ebenezer's work. It was a journey filled with laughter and excitement grew as the aircraft got closer to Israel.

It was late at night when the plane touched down at Ben Gurion airport. The *olim* were interviewed by Absorption Ministry officials before boarding two coaches for the drive to a hotel in Jerusalem, tired but very happy. The next morning the 'Red Carpet' programme began with a 'fair' in the same building. Various agencies offered all the necessary information about living in Israel – post office, banks, health service, phone companies, municipal and education services, tax, insurance and housing. This system had been designed to short-circuit the often lengthy process of absorption, enabling the *olim* to become settled more speedily than in the past.

Afterwards everyone went to the official welcoming ceremony at the *Kotel* (Western Wall). Following short speeches and singing of traditional Jewish songs came the emotional moment when each was given identity cards declaring they were now Israeli citizens. Another moving event was a festive dinner on Mount Scopus. Many were moved as Ken Hepworth told of how Ebenezer had helped bring nearly 130,000 Jewish people to the land from the former Soviet Union. He introduced Ebenezer's Olim Liaison Shirley Lawrenson, who has many years' experience of counselling and helping with emotional and humanitarian needs, utilising other Christian agencies as and when necessary.

Ebenezer supporters continue to be involved practically and financially with the Jewish Agency in supporting further UK *Aliyah* flights throughout 2010. As a result, it has been possible to form relationships and links with Jewish communities throughout the UK. The breakthrough had only come as a result of our partnership with the *aliyah* flights. Jeff believes the ministry is expanding – and only sees it getting busier. 'We need a structure of reps and prayer leaders in place, speaking into churches to broaden our supporter base and to raise our profile,' he said. 'The undergirding of prayer is vital.'

While the ministry of Ebenezer Operation Exodus has shifted gear into this wider vision for the Diaspora of the nations, their youth work leader Andy Ernst is concerned for the young people of this global Jewish community. His spiritual journey started as far back as his praying grandparents, who'd witnessed the rebirth of Israel from the ashes of the Holocaust. They believed something special was being fulfilled. They passed this understanding to their children – and their children's children. That included Andy.

'From the beginning of my involvement in Ebenezer fourteen years ago, I've seen myself as one representing the young adult population. I serve as a bridge builder between the generations.' His job title is International Young Adults Programme Co-ordinator for Operation Exodus – and his main aim is to equip the younger generations to carry on the work of *aliyah* to ensure the movement's future.

'It's been exciting to watch the younger generations of the nations rise up and take their place in the work of *aliyah*,' said Andy. 'The youth of the worldwide Body of Messiah is responding to the sound of the *shofar*.' In particular, Ebenezer has been seeing a growing interest in Israel among youth in non-western countries. 'Many among the young Christian generation in Latin American churches are on fire for God and are ready to serve Him. As we equip them with teaching and understanding, they'll become participants in preparing the way for the Jews to go home.'

Andy helps to do that by distributing materials, teaching young adult groups and sharing in youth conferences. Each year he and his team lead a group of young Christians from many different nations to Israel. This trip introduces the land and the people to participants. Through prayer times, practical serving, worship with local congregations, encounters with young Israelis as well as receiving profound biblical teaching on God's plan for Israel, the worldwide Church and Aliyah young Christians will be equipped to start blessing the Jewish people in their own country. This newly introduced programme *"engage"* offers the next generation a variety of possibilities to put their love for the Jewish people into action. The goal is to form local groups of young Christians to be involved with the work of Operation Exodus. Ministry and prayer trips through various countries to bless the Jewish population and to prepare Aliyah in prayer are taking place. 'The younger generations bring with them energy and vitality – and the elder people their wisdom and experience,' he explained. 'Each has his or her place and is interdependent. When we unite as the body – each with their unique contribution and expression – it is glorious.'

CHAPTER 11

A Path of Prayer

I have posted watchmen on your walls, O Jerusalem;
they will never be silent day or night.
You who call on the LORD, give yourselves no rest,
and give him no rest till he establishes Jerusalem
and makes her the praise of the earth.

Isaiah 62:6,7 (NIV)

They started with nothing. When Ebenezer emerged in 1991, the fledgling team had neither finances nor helpers. Yet nearly 20 years later, Christians in 40 countries are involved with the organisation.

Through its humanitarian aid work, so far Ebenezer has distributed many hundreds of tons of aid to needy people through its network of bases and representative offices. 'It's been dedicated teamwork involving volunteers and workers who've served faithfully over the years,' is how International Co-ordinator Alan Field put it, 'east and west working in partnership.'

Before joining Ebenezer in 1999, Alan held senior management and executive positions in the business world. He has also been involved in church leadership and church planting for more than 20 years. Alan became part of Ebenezer in 1999 and has since served in a number of leadership positions. He was appointed to his current role in September 2003 and is responsible for leading strategic change across the worldwide family of Ebenezer.

He is upbeat, as he reflects on the work so far. 'We've witnessed God's gracious and miraculous hand at work expanding the ministry in the nations,' he said. 'The Lord has also, once again, allowed us to pay every single bill and, although we have been tested at times, we entered 2010 without debt. At a time of world economic crisis, when many ministries are struggling, we can proclaim the Lord's faithfulness over our finances.'

Alan believes Ebenezer has a prophetic call to 'look and observe' what is happening on the world scene and to 'prayerfully discern' the signs of the time. 'We can see and feel we're living in times of shaking,' he pointed out. Yet there is a voice crying out in the wilderness of economic turmoil, tensions in world politics and escalating terrorism. It's the gentle voice of prayer: 'prepare the way of the Lord'.

'As we move forward, it will be ever more important to receive wisdom and to hear God's voice clearly,' said Alan. 'The work of *aliyah* must be Holy Spirit-led and the timing must always be God's choice. We need the ark of His presence to go before us and the cloud of the Holy Spirit to show us the way.'

Ebenezer Operation Exodus relies totally on prayer for the growth of its work. 'Intercession is at the heart of our ministry,' said Alan, 'and remains the bedrock of all we do. We must, as a high priority, continue to strengthen our network of intercessors worldwide – in each nation at the national, regional and local levels. I cannot emphasise strongly enough the importance of this objective.'

One of their champions in this area is Joan Thomas. Ever since she first became a Christian in 1967, Joan had 'an understanding' about the importance of Israel. 'Right from the first moment I began to pray,' she remembered of those early days, 'and I was always attending any meetings about Israel.' The teachings on Israel and prayer from Bible scholar Lance Lambert had a long lasting impact on her. Lance had founded Halford House Christian Fellowship in Richmond, England,

and had a deep understanding of these issues. Having discovered his own Jewish ancestry, Lance had become an Israeli citizen in 1980 and has his home in Jerusalem – his father and many members of his family died in the Holocaust.

Joan met Gustav Scheller in the mid 80s, and was present at the Jerusalem prayer conference that launched Ebenezer in 1991. She became International Prayer Co-ordinator in 1996. 'I've sought always to encourage prayer,' she said, stressing that she believes intercession in small groups is the 'backbone' of the ministry.

Ebenezer's pattern of prayer consists of a number of key elements. There has always been an understanding of the importance of using scripture in proclamation, and as a basis for prayer. Following the birth of the ministry, it was understood the priority was to prepare the *aliyah* highways through prayer, believing they would emerge at the right time for the Jewish people to go home. Isaiah 62:10 has been one of the key verses in this area:

> *Go through, go through the gates! Prepare the way for the people; Build up, Build up the highway! Take out the stones, lift up a banner for the peoples!*

As the operation has expanded over the years, special prayer journeys have been taken to prepare the way for the new work. Ebenezer's leaders and workers believe the Holy Spirit is emphasising the call to prepare the *aliyah* highways across nations in the worldwide Diaspora. Joan explained each prayer initiative/journey is different and undertaken only after thorough preparation and agreeing on the way forward. Every prayer journey must have the covering of the relevant Ebenezer leadership and, wherever possible, linked with the local church in the nation or region concerned. Joan and her colleagues trust God to help them identify spiritually significant sites.

'The *aliyah* highways need to be cleansed and any "stones" removed,' Joan explained. 'By "stones" I mean any obstacles and hindrances along the way which oppose *aliyah* such as – replacement theology, assimilation, historical and present-day anti-Semitism, idolatry, occult practices, and so on. Part of the understanding the Lord has given concerns the closing of false *aliyah* routes for the "true" gateways and highways to be open for Jewish immigrants to return to Israel.'

She cites one example – the initiative already mentioned by Australian Prayer Co-ordinator Philippa Kirk, where she explains the importance of prayer at internment camps in Hay, New South Wales, and Tatura, northern Victoria. 'This took place in 2009 and involved Australia, the UK, Gibraltar, the Republic of Ireland and Israel,' said Joan. 'It was a joint prayer action for the closing of false *aliyah* gateways to Australia – and the opening of the true *aliyah* gateways and highways to Israel.'

The background was researched in 2008. One of the UK prayer leaders found out about British convict ships transporting convicts to Australia between 1787 and 1868. Among their human cargo were Jewish immigrants who laid the foundations of the first Jewish community in Sydney. 'Subsequently free settlers progressively established a pilgrimage route,' said Joan, 'and present day evidence points to young Jewish families in the UK choosing to emigrate to Australia – rather than return to Israel.' Interestingly, even the Jewish Chronicle picked this up in April 2008, when they carried an article entitled, *Next year in...Sydney*. 'Israel is not the only popular destination for British Jews seeking a new life in the sun among others of their faith,' said the story. 'It may not quite be *aliyah* but Australia's pull is rising.'

This particular prayer initiative was new. For it involved people of five nations, with each team trusting God to guide their intercession, yet also keeping in close communication with one another. Prayer was prayed on agreed dates and times for co-ordinated action, with prayer teams in the associated nations at specific sites. Particular emphasis was at Portsmouth, England, as the first departure point for the sailings and Sydney, the destination. But there were other locations. Liverpool, England, had been the departure port for *HMT Dunera* in September 1940. The team there spent time at Woolfall Heath Estate, Huyton – the site of an 'enemy aliens' internment camp from 1939 to 1942.

The pattern of prayer and proclamation was followed through in each nation, with the final action on 11th July 2009. Exactly a month later, the first official Jewish Agency *aliyah* flight left the UK for Tel Aviv with 100 *olim* on board. Ebenezer had been asked by the JA in May 2009 to partner with them for this – with further flights to come. 'This prayer initiative saw the Lord breakthrough for UK *aliyah* to go forward in a new way,' said Joan. 'It was built on years of prayer from within Ebenezer and by believers over a long period of time who understood God's call to the Church to help His Jewish people return home.'

The path of prayer has taken them around Europe, too. Between 2004 and 2005, a prayer initiative had been launched to various key centres across Switzerland. Visiting Schaffhausen, the team walked along the German/Swiss border to a farm formerly used as a hiding place for Jews during World War II. Following Ebenezer's pattern of prayer, they asked God for forgiveness for the thousands of Jews who had been sent back from the border and ended up at concentration camps back in Germany. That team has been praying for a number of Jewish families to return to Israel, and so far have seen two young people from this region and some families from elsewhere in the country make the homecoming journey.

At Zurich, the group came upon the church where Ebenezer's founder Gustav Scheller had made his first steps of faith. They went on to the capital Berne, where they prayed at the local synagogue for the protection of the Jewish community there. They found out the federal government offices had been built on the site of a Jewish cemetery, and so said a prayer of confession and repentance. They stopped by the *Kindlifresser* – or 'child eater' – a grotesque fountain sculpture that depicts a Jewish man from the middle ages devouring Christian babies as part of so-called rituals. Suffice to say, the intercessors prayed for its removal.

Perhaps the most moving story from the Swiss initiative was when a 20-member team visited Zofingen. They'd found out that when pestilence hit Europe in 1348, Jews had been tortured at a place now called the 'Jewish Field'. After being forced to confess to poisoning the fountains, they were then burned at the stake. In commemoration of this grisly deed, the team carried a *menorah* to this field. Miraculously, the candles stayed lit despite wet weather. Prayers of confession and repentance were said, and tears flowed.

Praying for the *aliyah* from the nations is now an established part of Ebenezer's work. The shift took place at a UK conference in October 2000. Participants felt they were being guided to pray not only for the Jewish people in *'the land of the north'* – the former Soviet Union (fSU) – but also for those who'd settled elsewhere. 'Since this time,' said Joan, 'it's become increasingly clear that, while maintaining our commitment to watch over our operations in the fSU, we're also called to embrace a responsibility for the ingathering of Jewish people from the four corners of the worldwide Diaspora.'

International Chairman Markus Ernst was part of this change in Ebenezer's operations. He and wife Hanna had joined the ministry in 1996, after working in the business world. 'Someone sent us a tape where we heard Gustav speaking about flying over Siberia and expressing how he felt and what it meant,' Markus recalled. 'We were so touched. We prayed into this and Gustav came to Switzerland so we had a chance to meet him. He was asking for more people to develop the work there.' The Ernsts were part of a church that already had an understanding about the Jewish people and their part in God's plan for the world. So they had been primed for the ministry.

They witnessed the last sailing in 2004, and like everyone else, wondered where the work would go from there. 'The ministry of Ebenezer was recognised as "the one with the ship"' said Markus. 'Suddenly in 2004, the ship was gone.' But a growing conviction assured them it wasn't the end. 'The essence of it was that God was preparing the ministry for something bigger and greater than we'd experienced,' Markus explained. 'And we see it today, developing – that the *aliyah* is coming together from all nations.'

The prayer journey to Argentina in 2009 remains a highlight for him, and is a strong example of Ebenezer's commitment to the worldwide Diaspora. Twelve people from Switzerland visited the Latin American continent – as Markus put it – 'to pray against hindrances and to release the Jewish people to make *aliyah*'. A month or two after returning home, the intercessors received an e-mail saying that Ebenezer's Latin American team suddenly had many inquiries to share about *aliyah* in churches and synagogues. 'This showed us the power of intercession,' Markus explained. 'That's something we couldn't do. It's a real opening in God's timing.' Their experience has been confirmed by the Jewish Agency – a global partnership committed to bringing Jews home to Israel. They now work happily with Ebenezer around the world – which has been a wonderful breakthrough for the ministry. They have said they see Latin America as a major region for *aliyah*. 'So it's fitting together – which is exciting,' said Markus.

Elsa Scheller believes prayer is 'the power behind the work'. Widow of Ebenezer's founder, she looked back on the movement's history and said, 'I'm overwhelmed at what the Lord is doing – and in how many nations the work is taking off'. Admitting that the ministry has always been in 'battle stations' mode, she pointed out, 'That's why it's important we have these intercessors'.

Alongside prayer, she and Gustav also kept going because of a respect for their divine vocation. 'Gustav knew the Lord had called him,' Elsa remembered. 'He would say sometimes, "I know if I wouldn't do it, I'd be like Jonah. I would be swallowed up". The fear of God was there.' Their life together was a charming love story of a humble couple who sought to do the right thing – as they found themselves on the world stage, working with everyone from local dignitaries to government figures. 'I was a simple country girl,' said Elsa. 'My parents were farmers…And Gustav would say, "I'm just the Lord's donkey".' But they wanted more than success in the world's eyes. They craved significance in God's eyes. 'We need constantly to hear and know from the Lord,' said Elsa. 'We can run and run – but we might not be running His way if we're not aware of the Holy Spirit's guidance.'

Operation Exodus was born in Jerusalem in 1991 and celebrated its twentieth anniversary there in January 2011. During those twenty years, it has assisted more than 130,000 Jewish people from the fSU and elsewhere in the world to return to the land of Israel. Ebenezer Operation Exodus continues on that path. And they invite others to join them.

Text of Letter from Dr Kingsley Priddy of the Bible College of Wales:

At Eastbourne
22.ix.94

My dear Gustav and Elsa,

...God, the Holy Spirit, is in 'Operation Exodus' in a unique way. It is His own intercessory ministry for the return to Israel of the world's Jews. It is He who through this ministry is gaining a position of intercession which will prevail for the return of the ultimate remnant that is to be brought back from the four corners of the earth...

I remember your asking me some time ago to put something in writing with regard to the intercessory nature of 'Operation Exodus'. I did give some time to it then but somehow it never 'took off'; the Spirit did not give the liberty then, but I believe that now is His time.

You see, Intercession is not prayer, nor even very intense prayer. Anyone may pray, and pray earnestly, for something, and yet not be committed to be irrevocably responsible, at any cost, for its fulfilment. The intercessor is.

In Intercession there is Identification with the matter or persons interceded for. The intercessor is willing to take the place of the one prayed for; to let **their** need become **his** need;

to let **their** need be met at **his** expense and to let **their** suffering become the travail of **his** own heart.

That is how the Lord Jesus *'made intercession for the transgressors'* (Isaiah 53:12). *'He was numbered with the transgressors,'* and *'He was wounded for* (their) *transgressions'* (v.5). He had to be 'identified' with sinners; He secured their pardon by vicariously paying the debt that they owed.

He even went so far as to be *'made sin'* for us that we might be righteous in God's sight. He had to encounter everything that could ever come against us in the way of temptation, satanic opposition and such trials as abound in a fallen world. Whatever the devil was capable of he had to be free to bring it against the Lord Jesus. Jesus said to him, represented in his agents, *'This is your hour'* (Luke 22:53) when they came to arrest him.

'In all things He had to be made like His brethren ... to make propitiation for the sins of the people. For in that He himself has suffered being tempted, He is able to aid those who are tempted' (Hebrews 2:17–18).

And because *'the wages of sin is death,'* He had to partake of our flesh and blood *'that through death He might destroy him who had the power of death, that is, the devil, and release those who through fear of death were all their lifetime subject to bondage'* (Hebrews 2:14–15).

Only by such identification with sinners, even to suffering the very ultimate consequences of sin, in faultless victory, did our Lord gain that place of intercession for sinners which enabled Paul to throw out the challenge: *'Who is he who condemns? It is Christ who died, and is risen, who is even at the right hand of God, who also makes intercession for us'* (Romans 8:34).

And we are assured in Hebrews 7:25 that *'He is able to save to the uttermost those who come to God through Him, since He ever lives to make intercession for them.'*

The nearest anyone came to such a position under the Old Covenant was Moses, when he offered, if Israel's sin could be forgiven in no other way, to take their place and let God's judgment fall upon him. *'If you will forgive their sin – but if not, I pray, blot me out of your book which you have written'* (Exodus 32:32).

Others of the prophets became so identified with the nation that they could truly intercede for it. Even when Jeremiah felt the burden of the nation to be so heavy that he could never prophesy to it again, he found himself so in the grip of it, as fire shut up in his bones, that he could not hold it back (Jeremiah 20:8–9). Jeremiah was so identified with the nation that when, after the destruction of Jerusalem, the king of Babylon offered Jeremiah his liberty and protection, he chose to stay to minister to the remnant that were left, even when they disregarded the Lord's instructions and went off to Egypt (Jeremiah 43:4–7).

Esther was an intercessor when she laid her own life on the line, if by so doing her people might be saved (Esther 4:16).

Daniel's identification with the nation is clearly seen in Daniel 9 when everything else was put aside that he might cry to God for their return to their own land, in accordance with Jeremiah's prophecy. Not only did he prevail in this so that God was able to move Cyrus to fulfil it, but he had entered a spiritual realm in which God was able to reveal to him mysteries concerning the coming of Messiah and His atoning sacrifice (vv.20–27).

But mostly God looked in vain for such people. *'He saw that there was no man, and wondered that there was no intercessor'* (Isaiah 59:16). At a later time He said, *'I sought for a man among them who would make a wall, and stand in the gap before me on behalf of the land ... but I found no one'* (Ezekiel 22:30).

In this dispensation it is the Holy Spirit Himself who is the true intercessor on earth. *'The Spirit himself makes intercession for us with groanings which cannot be uttered ... He makes intercession for the saints according to the will of God'* (Romans 8:26–27).

But He has limited Himself to exercising this ministry

through redeemed men (or women) who have allowed Him to indwell their bodies as His temples (1 Corinthians 6:19). He would be quenched if there were any tension or conflict between His will and theirs, which necessitates such a surrender of the believer's will that his body can be presented to God as *'a living sacrifice'* (Romans 12:1).

Then there is a daily dying to self-will that the Holy Spirit may be free to live **His** life within that body. As Paul said, *'We who live are always delivered to death for Jesus' sake, that the life of Jesus may be manifested in our mortal flesh. So then death is working in us, but life in you'* (2 Corinthians 4:11–12). It is a costly, but glorious, ministry.

So the human channel becomes increasingly identified with the indwelling Spirit, as they both jointly become identified with the one for whom intercession is being made.

The pain and trials that are experienced are partly because thereby the natural life still remaining in the human instrument – elements of pride, selfishness, stubbornness, jealousy etc. – may be put to death, *'crucified with Christ'* (Galatians 2:20), and be replaced by *'the new man, created according to God in righteousness and true holiness'* (Ephesians 4:24).

God's way is always the way of the cross for it is only through death that resurrection life can be realised. *'Unless an ear of wheat falls into the ground and dies, it remains alone; but if it dies, it produces much fruit'* (John 12:24).

Even in a matter which has been given by God and is in accordance with the will of God, if great success and prosperity follow it is impossible for the human instrument not to take some pride or credit, even if only in thought, unless that element in him has truly died. That is why it seems to be inevitable that at some stages the work of God will seem to go to death, that the one to be used will know truly what an inadequate failure he is and then, when God ultimately brings resurrection and gives the victory, His channel will never touch the glory even in thought.

But pain and trials are also experienced because the accomplishing of God's will is always opposed by the devil. His agents will certainly contest the work of God and use every means available to do so.

The Spirit through His instruments must repel and defeat every such attack by laying hold of Calvary's once-and-for-all victory and applying it through faith and obedience, using *'the sword of the Spirit, which is the word of God.'* As the enemy is overcome at every point a victory is established which can subsequently be applied again in similar circumstances. This is gaining a position of intercession from which intercession may be made in future.

Thus it is that, from His once-and-for-all victory gained at Calvary, the Lord Jesus *'ever lives to make intercession for'* every sinner who will come to God through Him.

It is in such a manner that the Holy Spirit is using 'Operation Exodus' to gain a position of intercession for the subsequent return of the Jews from every part of the world. Although that is clearly foretold in Scripture and is certain of fulfilment, it will not happen automatically.

God foretold through Jeremiah that the Jews would return from Babylon after seventy years, but it necessitated the intercession of Daniel when that time came to bring its fulfilment.

Although our Lord said that *'this gospel of the kingdom will be preached in all the world as a witness to all the people groups'* before the end will come, the Holy Spirit will not be able to do that without the lives of multitudes of the saints being sacrificially placed at His disposal.

In the course of 'Operation Exodus' the devil must be allowed to bring every kind of opposition against it that he can devise. But as, through faith and costly obedience by His channels, the Holy Spirit overcomes every one of these, every weapon that the enemy could use to prevent the full second exodus from taking place will already have been blunted or broken. So he will be powerless to prevent that mighty surge of the Spirit when His time comes to complete His final *aliyah* from the four quarters of the globe...

It is a great privilege, but a very costly one, for Gustav and Elsa, and all who will be 100% involved with them, to be the Holy Spirit's prepared instruments for this end-time intercessory ministry. They will need and deserve all the support that the rest of us can give in prayer and other ways.

Shalom!

Yours in His love and triumph,

Kingsley

Bible References

Prophecies of God's Word:
Genesis 12:1–3
Genesis 35:11–12
Jeremiah 23:3–8
Jeremiah 30:10
Ezekiel 20:33–35
Ezekiel 36:17-28
Zephaniah 2:1–2

Performance of God's Word:
Isaiah 49:22
Isaiah 59:21
Jeremiah 31:37
Ezekiel 36
Romans 11:11–12, 17–18, 25–31
Romans 15:27
Ephesians 3:6

General References for further study:
Deuteronomy 4:27
Deuteronomy 28:64a
Deuteronomy 30:1–4
Deuteronomy 32:26
Psalm 105:37, 42–43
Psalm 106:44–47

Psalm 122:6
Psalm 137:4–6
Psalm 147:2-3
Isaiah 11:10–12
Isaiah 14:1–2
Isaiah 27:12–13
Isaiah 35:8–10
Isaiah 40:1–5
Isaiah 41:8–11
Isaiah 42:22
Isaiah 43:1, 2, 6, 8, 13
Isaiah 44:3–6
Isaiah 45:2–6
Isaiah 46:3–4
Isaiah 49:8–10
Isaiah 51:14
Isaiah 57:14, 18
Isaiah 60:4, 8–9
Isaiah 62:4–7, 10–12
Jeremiah 13:16–18
Jeremiah 16:14–15
Jeremiah 23:3, 7–8
Jeremiah 30:16–17
Jeremiah 31:7–11, 31–34
Ezekiel 34:11–13, 16
Ezekiel 36:8, 24–28
Ezekiel 37:12–14
Ezekiel 39:27–28
Hosea, chapters 3, 4, 11, 14
Amos 9:11–15
Micah 4:6–7
Zephaniah 2:6–7
Romans 15:27

Letters from the Knesset and Jewish Agency

IMMIGRATION & ABSORPTION
COMMITTEE

הכנסת
KNESSET

Jerusalem, 20 January 1992
15 Shevat 5752

Ebenezer Emergency Fund
EXODUS II
Ebenezer House
5a Poole Road
Bournemouth
ENGLAND

Dear Friends,

I have followed with great interest the establishment of the EXODUS SHIPPING LINE. On behalf of the Immigration and Absorption Committee of the Knesset, I am extending to you our sincere congratulations on the successful completion of the first three sailings from Odessa to Haifa.

I am well aware of all your efforts which have made these historic sailings possible and I have been deeply touched by the generous donations from Christians around the world. It is good to see Israel has so many friends who care about the return of our people from the land of the North.

My good wishes accompany EEF/EXODUS II, and may, through your efforts, many thousands of Soviet Jews find their way home.

Yours sincerely,

Michael Kleiner, M.K.
Chairman

הסוכנות היהודית לארץ־ישראל
The Jewish Agency for Israel

המחלקה לעליה וקליטה

Department of Immigration
and Absorption

August 19, 1993

לשכת ראש המחלקה
Office of the Head of
the Department

2 7 AUG 1993

Mr. Gustav Scheller
International Coordinator
Ebenezer Emergency Fund
Ebenezer House
5a Poole Road
Bournemouth BH2 5QJ
ENGLAND

Dear Mr. Scheller,

I was very impressed with your personality and your words at
the Knesset in Jerusalem. We very much appreciate what you
are doing for the Jewish people and the State of Israel.

I would also like to extend our appreciation to your sponsors.
You are part of a great historic event, the ingathering of the
Jewish people to their land. Thank you for what you are
doing.

Very truly yours,

Uri Gordon
Head, Department of
Immigration and Absorption

JERUSALEM, P.O.B. 92 ירושלים ת״ד
Tel: 02-202537-8 טל׳   Fax: 02-202251 פקס.
TEL-AVIV, 17 Kaplan Street – Tel. 03-5423450-690 טל׳ – 17 רח׳ קפלן ,תל־אביב

Getting Involved

Is God challenging you to be involved in Operation Exodus? For more information about this, and to find out about supporting financially and in prayer, please contact the nearest office from the list below.

UK (Head Office)
Ebenezer Emergency Fund International
Ebenezer House
5a Poole Road
Bournemouth, BH2 5QJ
UK
Tel: +44 (0)1202 294455
Email: enquiries@ebenezer-ef.org
Website: www.operation-exodus.org

Australia & South East Asia Oceania
Operation Exodus SE Asia Oceania
Level 2, 39 Leighton Place
Hornsby
NSW 2077
Australia
Tel: + 61 2 9482 4692
Email: office@operation-exodus-seao.org
Website: www.operation-exodus-seao.org

Canada
Operation Exodus Canada
Suite #456
7184 – 120th Street
Surrey, BC
V3W 0M6
Canada
Email: canada@ebenezer-ef.org

New Zealand
Ebenezer Emergency Fund
PO Box 5319
Terrace End
Palmerston North 4441
New Zealand
Tel: +64 6357 4883
Email: ebenezernz@xtra.co.nz

South Africa
Ebenezer Emergency Fund South Africa
PO Box 61887
Vaalpark, 1948
South Africa
Tel: +27 169 711 766
Email: southafrica@ebenezer-ef.org

USA
Ebenezer Emergency Fund USA
PO Box 568
Lancaster
NY. 14086
USA
Tel: +1 716 681 6300
Email: info@ebenezerusa.org
Website: www.ebenezerusa.org